GET YOUR NAME ON COOL STUFF

Mark Basford

Notice

Get Your Name on Cool Stuff. First edition.
2015
ISBN: 978 -988-14152-1-9

Published by Mark Richard Basford in Hong Kong

CONTENTS

ACKNOWLEDGEMENT

This is my first book, and had it not been for the active support of two very special groups of people, I would never have written it.

First, to my lovely family - Kate, Isabelle, Tom, and Nick - thank you so much for your continued love, understanding, support, and patience over the last few months whilst Dad has been "Doing The Book".

Secondly, I want to give a big shout-out to the PnP community – you know who you are! Without your inspiration, encouragements, advice, and support I'd never have made it either.

Thanks all!

DEDICATION

For Pat and Dick

MARK BASFORD

ENDORSEMENTS FOR MARK BASFORD AND SYNCO MARKETING

"Mark and the Synco team have been highly effective in meeting our promotional product needs. They have been eager to accommodate changes in designs whilst giving valuable input when needed. The quality has been fantastic and we will continue to work with them in the future. I would happily recommend Mark to others."

Director, Financial Services, Hong Kong

"We tasked Synco Marketing with the job of designing and supplying hundreds of good quality conference pens and folders for a series of regional events. Their service and product turned out to be just what we wanted and the folders were a hit - there are none left"

Regional Marketing Leader Asia,
Leading Global HR Solutions Provider Hong Kong

"We ordered hats from Mark at Synco Marketing to help us with fund-raising and awareness of our non-profit organisation - we're delighted with their service and the products! Our logo looks great on the caps, and we've already started selling them. Thanks for your help!"

Non-Profit Organisation
Hong Kong

"We asked Synco Marketing to make an initial small order for some caps to promote our new brand - they look great, really happy with them. Also, we like the straight forward business during the meetings. Thank you!"

Owner / Director Fine Food Importer
Hong Kong

"We need top quality products for attendee gifts at our annual Asia conference. Mark and the Synco team came up with great suggestions – and the leather card case we selected turned out to be a really popular choice. We even had senior partners from our New York head office asking for extras to take back home!"

APAC Business Development head,
International Law Firm, Hong Kong

"Mark at Synco Marketing provided us with many great design ideas for our corporate branded wristbands for a rugby event. They delivered a high quality product on budget, and under a very tight deadline. The wristbands were a big hit, and working with Synco was most enjoyable and worry-free!"

Marketing Manager,
International Law Firm, Hong Kong

"We highly appreciated Synco's help to make our polo shirts in a short period with good quality and on-time delivery. Your staff was also very helpful with providing some suggestions to make our polo shirts look great. Definitely will come back to you when we have our next order."

Management Consultants,
Hong Kong

"It was a pleasure doing business with you Mark, and we will continue to do so for future orders and College requirements.

From the moment we contacted you with our request, to the time the items arrived, all correspondence has been seamless and efficient. Your professional approach and "nothing is too difficult" attitude has made this a very easy exercise, considering we are located in Australia.

Thank you once again for your advice, professionalism, and prompt service. We will certainly have no hesitation in utilising your company for future marketing projects and recommending Synco Marketing Ltd. to our Colleagues."

School Administrator, Queensland, NSW

FOREWORD

By Trevor Smith: Executive Coach, ACC, APFS, CFP™, CEO
and Founder of The Orchard Partnership

Whatever the occasion, we all love to receive gifts.

Over the past 30 years, I've lost track of the number of corporate branded goodies I've given out, and occasionally received. I've seen great results from some of those campaigns, and I often wonder how long my valued clients kept or remembered those promotional items.

Yet at the same time, some of the things I received really missed the mark.

Millions of dollars potentially wasted.

Yet for me, there is one gift I received that really stands out.

Fifteen years ago, I managed to qualify for an achievers' convention. The organisers handed me a personalised Swiss multi- tool. Wow! How did they know this was exactly what I wanted? Care and consideration had gone into this gift, to the extent that I still remember the giver, and I am in touch with him today. When some years later the multi-tool vanished in a house move, I willingly spent my own money to replace it.

This is the power of a well-selected promotional item. It touches the heart and soul of the recipient.

Clients of Mark Basford know the care and attention he puts into getting this right. He makes sure his clients get maximum bang for their buck. Why do I know this? Because I am one of those clients.

Mark Basford's "Get Your Name on Cool Stuff" is a book for people who want to take action – and attract new customers, build loyalty, and increase their profits.

If you're looking to make a big noise in your market through well-targeted and impactful promotional items, and you're ready to get stuck in now to learn what it takes to be the Promo Products Pro in your organisation – this book is for you.

Originally from the UK, Trevor Smith is qualified as an Associate of the Chartered Insurance Institute (ACII) and a 'Chartered Insurer', 'Associate of the Personal Finance Society' (AFPS) and 'Certified Financial Planner' CFP.

He has achieved the 'Accreditation in Executive Coaching' (Level 3) from the Institute of Executive Coaching (Aus) and is accredited by the International Coach Federation (ICF) as an 'Associate Certified Coach'.

INTRODUCTION

Dear Friend,

Welcome to **Get Your Name on Cool Stuff – The Ultimate Guide to Attracting New Customers, Building Loyalty, and Increasing Profits with Promotional Product Marketing.**

This book has been inside my head trying to come out for a long time. I've spent more than 25 years in marketing and sales, and I've seen Promotional Products all over the world - used well and used badly. I've been fascinated and amazed by their power, and irritated and frustrated beyond belief by the crazy things that can go wrong.

I've been proud to call Hong Kong my home for the last 16 years or so. I love the buzz and the excitement of the city, and it is a fantastic and energizing place to build a business. My company Synco Marketing was set up to offer great service to marketing people and entrepreneurs who needed straightforward professional guidance and a pain-free, reliable supply of great Promotional Products that really work for them. We've built an incredible team here, and had the privilege of working with some great clients along the way. Maybe you are one of them? – if so, thank you!

I want to explain a little more about the format of the book. It's particularly important to me that you can feel that this book is more than a one-off read – it's actually intended to be interactive and a starting point for us to build some mutual understanding.

There are lots of additional resources linked to the book, and the idea is that you can access these at the same time whilst you are absorbing the content you find in the book. It's a way for you to dig further into the content, and to register to get updates to the book as it is expanded or modified to take account of new ideas, research, and findings. We live in a fast-moving world, and it's easy for a writer nowadays to update their content, so don't miss out - sign up to be sure to get the new versions and revisions as they are published, and for access to all the other bonus materials like PDFs printable checklists, videos, and so on.

I've read the text over and over and had it edited many times, but of course it's always possible for typos, grammatical errors, and other mistakes to creep in. So I do also want to ask you to PLEASE let me know about any mistakes you can find. Just send the details of any error and the page number to my email mark@syncomarketing.com so I can make sure the book stays as accurate – and as easy to read - as possible.

It's also important to be clear that this book is primarily intended for business people.

For entrepreneurs involved in growing one or more businesses they own themselves, free to decide on their own course of actions, but feeling pressure to get better results from limited resources.

Or for people working in a large company in a marketing and sales role, looking to be more personally effective in spite of corporate inertia, and trying to balance different viewpoints and agendas.

I've been in both of those positions, and understand the pressures and pleasures of each!

I should also say that this book is for people who want to take action. It's not going to give you the answers to *what* to do, but it will help you work through what's right for you in your situation. And it will show you how you personally can become more successful in this specialized area of marketing.

You'll sense by now that this book was never intended to become a High Street bookstore bestseller. First, it's targeted at people like you who have a very specific need to make this element of marketing work better for them - and secondly, it's really designed to open a conversation with you, to give us a chance to know each other better, to develop trust and respect, and to make some connection which could help us decide if one day it would make sense for us to work together.

I can't deny that I'm a passionate promoter and believer in the power of marketing using Promotional Products – and I'm not averse to a bit of shameless self-promotion myself at the same time. Of course, I want you to get more customers, build loyalty, and improve your profits using Promotional Product Marketing, and for sure, reading this book is one of the ways you can start to do that. But in addition to this, and as a complement to the material in the book, you'll find lots of opportunities here to register to watch videos, download additional information, checklists, and so on.

And of course I'd love to become your preferred Promo Products Specialist adviser and supplier, and work with you to Get Your Name on some of the Cool Stuff we have on offer - products which really work, and which will make your life easier as a result.

If you find you don't like the book, that's OK too. I'll be happy to arrange for a refund of your purchase price – please forward your receipt to mark@syncomarketing.com, and we'll arrange a refund. Of course I'd prefer you to not leave a negative review just because you don't like my punctuation, my spelling, or the way I say what I want to say – just drop me a private email to let me know this is not for you, and we'll arrange that refund and part company just as friends who see things differently. Thanks!

On the other hand, if you DO like what you read, I'd really love to hear from you so I can get to know you better, and have a chance to learn what you found useful in the book, and what else you'd like to hear about in future updates – visit the weblink below to register and I'll be back in touch. Or you could post a picture or a comment on Facebook at www.facebook.com/syncomarketing

Thanks again for getting hold of my book, I'm really looking forward to getting to know you better.

Sincerely

Mark Basford

Discovery Bay, Hong Kong 2015

This book is interactive - to get free updates and bonus videos, access to more resources and upgrades to this book when new versions or editions are released

Visit www.getyournameoncoolstuff.com

or scan this QR code

and follow the instructions

CHAPTER ONE

What Is Promotional Product Marketing, And Why Does It Work?

I've conducted lots of surveys asking people about the best promotional items they've received and more often than not, people are able to easily recall something that they really liked. Surprisingly, very often what springs to mind is a gift they received a good few years ago.

Personally, I use a travel wallet that was given to me by a colleague who worked in the steel industry in Canada. I've never been to Canada, nor needed to buy steel there, (and I've been given other wallets), but 18 years after I was given that wallet, I'm still using it, and Dofasco is the only company I can name in the Canadian steel industry without hesitation.

Dofasco since became a part of a big steel group, Arcelor Mittal, but the Dofasco name still lives on. Even though the logo on my wallet doesn't reflect that change, I don't feel I need an updated wallet, and it doesn't affect how I feel about the company at all. Most importantly, I've never bought a single kilo of steel from them, but if anyone were to ask me about a steel company in Canada, Dofasco would be the first name I'd mention.

So a gift that cost a few dollars builds goodwill with a steel industry colleague and secured ongoing personal endorsement for nearly two decades (and counting).

Not only that, I've mentioned the Dofasco name to you too.

That was five times in the 30 seconds it took you to read the last three paragraphs.

That wallet continues to work for Dofasco after nearly twenty years. That's a long-lasting impact!

In this chapter I'm going to explain what Promotional Product Marketing is, what Promotional Products are, and why you need them.

I'll describe why you should consider it as an investment to achieve your business objectives, and explain why it works so well.

What is Promotional Product Marketing?

Let's start out by being really clear about what we mean by Promotional Product Marketing.

If you're thinking of "promotions", by which I mean tactics like price-cutting initiatives, or campaigns using money-off coupons, or Buy One Get One Free campaigns (or BOGOFs) to market a company's products, then think again. There's a whole lot of literature out there that deals with this –but that's not what we're about here.

The Promotional Product Marketing I'm describing in Get Your Name on Cool Stuff is something quite different. Here I'm talking about using Promotional Products, branded corporate gifts, company souvenirs, or another free item (which in most cases would not be the core product your company supplies) to deliver a message about your company, products, or services so as to help you achieve a specific business objective or deliver a certain outcome.

One of these specific business objectives *might* be to "sell more" of your company's own products or services, but there are many other business objectives where Promotional Product Marketing can legitimately help too. I'll be talking about these a little further on in the book.

What Are "Promotional Products"?

Popular Promotional Products are things we're all familiar with - if you take a look around your workspace, there's a strong chance that there will be two or three branded promotional items sitting on your desk right now. Maybe a USB thumb drive, maybe a pen, maybe some sticky notes or a notebook, each of these showing a company logo or brand name printed on it.

I've been running an ongoing survey with my contacts over the last year or so, and the results from this show that two out of three people have promo products within sight of their personal workspace. In fact, more than 25% of those surveyed had three or more products on their desk. If you'd like to take part in the survey too, please go to http://www.supersimplesurvey.com/Survey/6922/Hi_there_Mark_here/

From an industry supply point of view, the most popular products are branded pens (over a billion pens a year are produced for the U.S. market alone) - and T-shirts, which account for the highest sales value.

As a marketer, it's very tempting to get initially distracted by just focusing on the Cool Stuff, and to get stuck straight into choosing a product right away. This in itself proves how attractive and enticing promotional products really are – however, this is where marketers, and even some experienced entrepreneurs, should hold back and rewind the process a little.

Choosing the Product itself is actually the last part of the puzzle.

Why do I need Promotional Products? - they won't work for my industry / company / situation

First, let's deal with one issue - I've heard people tell me with great confidence that promotional products **don't work** for their industry, or that they simply **don't need** them.

I respect that view - it could very well be that they are right, and their own success has led them to believe that their way is THE way, and they don't actually need any help. They're already doing very well thank you, and are pretty happy with the way things are right now.

In this case, it's pretty unlikely that they'll be reading this book, and I don't think they're likely to be changing their mind any day soon.

My guess is that if, instead of Promotional Products, I told them that I was in the printed media advertising business, or in direct mail, or in outbound email marketing, then these people would probably tell me that those things also don't work for their industry or that they just don't need them.

To be brutally honest, it really doesn't matter what business you are in, if you don't feel you need any help, then you're right, you probably don't need any help (...until the time comes when you realise that you do).

For that reason, in fact, I rarely spend much time trying to convince the inconvincible – my time's pretty limited too, and I prefer to just move on and work with action-orientated people who GET IT.

But if you're someone who does need to make something different happen in your business, if you have an objective you need help reaching – even something as apparently straightforward as "making sure your target market knows that you've arrived and that you're here, ready to help, right NOW" – and you think that you could do with some help, then for sure you should look into Promotional Products.

It's basically the same for any industry - professional services, entertainment, media, event management, F+B outlets, exhibitions, agriculture, retail, clubs and associations, heavy industry, funeral parlours – in fact if you can tell me about a business area where Promotional Product Marketing can't help, please email me at mark@ syncomarketing.com and let me know so I can include it in the next edition of this book.

So in short, NO! You don't need to use Promotional Products, but in the same way that you don't need to use outbound email marketing, or social media, or host events, or have a website, or print a brochure, if you choose not to use them, you might be missing a trick.

So let's leave the products themselves to one side for a moment, and think about making an investment

An Investment to Achieve your Business Objectives

The only sound business reason for using Promotional Products is to help you achieve a business objective.

- It's not about having some freebies to hand out at a trade show.
- It's not about having a stock cupboard full of giveaways just in case somebody wants something.
- It's not about "just getting our name out there".
- It's not about buying some umbrellas to "get ourselves noticed when people look down out of their office blocks, when it's raining".

Whilst some of these might be "nice outcomes", these shouldn't be the *reasons* you use for investing in Promotional Product Marketing. And some of them might not actually help you very much, or at all!

Campaigns

It's time to start thinking of Promotional Products in terms of Campaigns, just like any other type of advertising – one where the "benefit" generated by the Campaign exceeds the "costs" of running it.

You're investing some of your company's money

- in a Campaign
- to help you achieve a specific objective
- to see a positive return on that investment.

In fact, this is no different than any other type of company expenditure – whether it's advertising or something else.

Think about it…

- You wouldn't advertise in a magazine unless you believed that you would make more in sales than the cost of the ad.
- You wouldn't sign off on an employee's application for an airfare to a distant location unless you believed that there was a strong chance that her trip would generate future profits in excess of the cost of the flight.
- You wouldn't sanction the purchase of additional raw materials for a client-specific order unless you strongly believed that there was a profitable order in the pipeline.

Well, ok, I'm realistic enough to know that sometimes these things *do* happen in the corporate world, but that's not to say that they *should* happen. For sure, we're not always totally rational in our approach to life or work decisions, and yes, sometimes you do need to make an entrepreneurial judgement call (or "take a risk", depending on how you look at these things).

As a responsible business owner or executive, you'd want to be sure that any spending on which you're signing off is justified, and has a good chance of generating a positive return.

So just like any other type of expenditure in your company, there should be a clear understanding of two things

1) why you are spending the cash, and
2) some sort of calculation to verify that the money spent will generate a greater benefit when compared to alternative ways you might use that money (like hiring more staff or leaving it in the bank).

When you adopt the mindset where you think of Promotional Products as a tool to help you achieve your business objectives, it all starts to make a lot more sense.

So if it's about investing in a campaign to help achieve a business objective – it's going to be really important to clearly define the specific business objective that you're trying to achieve.

Which business objectives are we talking about?

Promotional Product Marketing can help achieve many different business objectives.

Some examples:–

Attracting New Customers

- Client acquisition programmes
- Encouraging referrals
- Trade fair attendance
- Outreach programmes

Building Loyalty

- Finding ways to get your existing clients to love you more, so that they will help you increase your turnover as they buy again, and buy more when you cross-sell.
- Turning clients into open and sympathetic buyers of new related products.
- Keeping in touch – with "thank you" gifts and updates.
- Building better relationships internally with staff or with suppliers, so that they support you as you grow.

Improving Profits

- Using promotional items as direct ways to generate more sales.
- Creating an environment where there is less resistance to price increases.
- Improving operational efficiency through reduced organisational costs, and lower staff turnover.

Promotional Products can play a part in any of these strategies – initially as part of your client acquisition programme, then to publicise and build awareness of your initiatives, and finally to actively encourage and incentivise people to behave in the way which generates your desired outcome.

Why Promotional Product Marketing works so well

What you really need to know about Promotional Product Marketing can be summarized in three words

It. Really. Works.

It really works because… it's Physical

The key word in Promotional Product Marketing is "PRODUCT". A physical product is something tangible, something you can hold in your hand or touch – and as such, it engages more of the five physical senses than sight alone. Often, there's a subtle excitement of the other senses too – think about the smell of a new leather item like a business card wallet, or the taste of chocolate in a promotional confectionary item. Even sound works too – you can hear a pen click, the crinkly noise of a polythene bag containing a smart new polo shirt, or the noise the waterproof zipper makes on a top quality backpack, or the snap of elastic on a new notebook cover.

Product marketers have known this for a long time - the visual aspect of a product is a crucial trigger for sales, but it's not the only one. Sight accounts for only up to 60% of the time in the consumer's decision to buy. Once the visual elements of the product have been fully exploited, different sensory aspects come into play. Researchers have found that smell is the next important sense to appeal to a consumer followed by sound, taste, and touch, in that order of importance. Multisensory elements on products, therefore, send signals that the brain converts into buying impulses.

What's more, it's believed that multi-sensory impressions stimulate right brain activity – the part of the brain that responds emotionally to stimuli, rather than the more logical left brain. So brand recognition and the urge to purchase which follows is more of an emotional task as opposed to a logic-based task for the brain.

Online shopping is undoubtedly popular, often straightforward, and arguably a more efficient use of your precious time than aimlessly wandering up and down the High Street. But as a High Street consumer, you get to see and feel the physicality of the products you are considering – which stimulates all the senses - and this generates more emotional responses.

If you'd like to read a little more about this and see some links to research, register at www.getyournameoncoolstuff.com for the bonuses that come with the book, and download the Multisensory Stimulation And Brand Recall white paper from the Membership page.

You'll know all about this already if your company designs and sells physical products – because if you can't generate a positive emotional response with your own company products, then you won't sell many.

However, if you are in Professional Services, like Law, Accountancy, or Consulting, or if you operate a manufacturing plant or sell raw materials, or perhaps make another product which doesn't fit the High Street model – how can you generate that same sort of emotional reaction in your prospects and clients?

This is where Promotional Products step in, as the substitute (or additional) physical product for people to associate with your brand.

For sure, traditional advertising, phone calls, emails and direct mail, and person-to-person meetings all play a part in that sequence of multiple contacts or events needed to build confidence. But if you can directly associate your company name or message with some sort of multi-dimensional product – something they can hold in their hand - you'll help to generate a more emotional response, and dramatically increase your impact.

Today, so much of our time at work is spent dealing with two-dimensional and purely visual features – we see everything on a flat screen. In many ways, particularly at work, we've forgotten the importance of sensory impact.

Have you noticed how you get a sensory boost when you can hold something in your hands and move it around? Touching something, feeling something, holding something, somehow just makes things feel more real. Looking at an object whilst touching it at the same time increases brain activity dramatically, and this makes it easier for messages connected with the experience to be received and retained.

What's more, it's a natural human response to crave this!

There's lots of everyday evidence to support this – look around the exhibits at a busy museum – the queues are for the "have a go" hands-on exhibits not the "look and read" ones.

You should see the reaction when we deliver a new batch of polo shirts or pens to a client. It's just the same as at the museum - people crowd around to look, touch, and feel that new Cool Stuff!

It really works because… it's got Long-lasting impact

Impact is crucial to marketing success - everyone wants to have more impact than their competition. So simply having a few good promotional products in your company or organisation's tool kit to give to clients and prospects immediately gives you an edge over any competitor who might think that Promotional Product Marketing is a waste of time, and can't be bothered to do it.

Putting your name on something is making a statement with impact– you're validating yourself. It's almost a way to "prove" to the world that you're really there.

Remember how as children we all had the urge to make an impact with our name? We'd write our name on things to show they belong to us - and by doing this, we'd be showing to everyone else that we're significant and important in our world.

Big brands and large companies do just the same – they all put their names on things too. They do this because they know that this helps us to perceive them as being real, or somehow more present, even when their own products aren't there, and the memory of them will work on our subconscious and increase the chance of recall when we get to the buying point.

Smaller companies who may be some way outside the public eye also like to put their name on things too - as a very legitimate way to underline and assert the fact that they are "real" too (just like the big companies we've heard of).

They're saying, "Hey look at us! We're more than just a website and a guy in his spare bedroom. Our company is significant; we're something to be recognised and to be reckoned with. We're serious, take us seriously too".

You can get great impact with traditional advertising such as media print ads – however, you need to pay for a large number of these to get that impact, because you've only got a short time before it's literally yesterday's news, and then you need to run the campaign again.

However, if you are looking for impact which lasts longer, then Promotional Products really come to the fore. We're talking about great campaigns, ones using products that will sit on a client's desk for years, or live happily in a customer's home for decades. You just can't get that with a print ad in Wednesday's newspaper.

The best Promotional Products will keep working for a very long time - that's because people really do keep hold of gifts which are well-designed, work well, and prove to be useful in some way. In my survey, more than half of the respondents said the best promo item they had received was given to them longer than a year ago. Not only that, even though these gifts were "old", the impact was still working. An impressive 95% of respondents could still remember the company name associated with their favourite product.

I've got a coffee mug I use at home today that is imprinted with my favourite football team's logo on it – I got it in 1973, and it's still going strong – it's in almost daily use.

I've also got a much-treasured pack of playing cards my mother was given when she flew home to England from Venezuela with Aer Lingus. She made that trip in 1950, so at the time of writing that means 65 years of branding impact for that airline in our family so far, and counting– we still use them today.

I bet there's more Cool Stuff like this in your home or office too. If you've got a classic promo product at home, please feel free to share it with us on our Facebook page www.facebook.com/syncomarketing

It really works because… it represents Great Value for Money

In terms of cost per view, Promo Products can be amazingly competitive. My mother's Aer Lingus playing cards have proven to be a low-cost long-lasting product for that company, giving exposure to their brand for well over half a century. But as a simpler example, consider a desktop calendar, ideally one that has three-dimensional touch-and-feel aspects which makes it irresistible to fiddle about with!

Let's assume that a physical desktop calendar is viewed on average 10 times a day in the average workplace – as a rough calculation, that's 2,000 views in a typical work year of 200 office days.

Now, although it's going to cost you a few dollars to buy 500 calendars and ship them out to your clients and prospects in the first place, if you divide that total cost by the 2000 views (or "impressions") you can expect to get from each one, the resultant cost per impression is tiny. Of course, you've got to be sure that your calendar makes it past the recycling bin when it arrives on your client's desk the first time, but that's another story.

So if the business objective that you're trying to achieve is to "make it easy and natural for my clients to find my name on their desk when they need my services later this year", then using a calendar could be a great value-for-money solution.

It really works because… it's easily Targeted

With print advertising, you can target a general demographic based on the type of magazine they read. But you can't be sure that the people who make up this demographic will notice your ad, and you can't pinpoint an approach to specific individuals.

At a trade show, you can give out your generic company brochure to everyone who passes your booth. But if that's all you have with you, you're missing out on a chance to make a deeper impression with the real VIP prospects you meet. They'll just have to make do with the brochure like everyone else.

TV and radio can work for local businesses as well as larger national and international brands, though the entry costs can be high, particularly for TV, and as with print advertising, it's only a general approach to a demographic. For some businesses, this targeting may not be specific enough, especially those looking to reach a smaller number of corporate clients.

When you use Promo Product Marketing, you can engineer the distribution of your Cool Stuff so that you have better control over who gets your Products. This way you can tailor your campaign to suit the expected audience, and target it very specifically at individuals in a personalized way.

It really works because… it's super-Flexible

I always recommend clients to focus on their specific campaign objectives in order to define the right Promotional Product to suit their needs. However, promotional products are amazingly flexible, and you can use one item in more than one way.

Think of the multiple uses of a coffee mug – as a direct call to one person to read a message printed on the outside (or that more personal handwritten note you put inside), or as longer-term impact branding when you give a whole batch of them to your client to put in their pantry area. You could also use a mug as packaging, perhaps for sweets or other food treats when you want to say thank you to someone, whilst at the same time giving something that will last longer than the time they take to consume it.

Or you can use different items in isolation or in various combinations to achieve differentiation between tiers of recipients. For example, just using one or two items– for example, notebooks and pens – and varying how you present or deliver them, allows you to arrange suitable gifts for different levels of contact. Prospects might receive a pen as an incentive when they sign up for your mailing list, whilst visitors to your seminar might receive only the notebook. You could reserve the dual product "pen and notebook combo" as a set which you offer in a good quality presentation box, perhaps with a personalized thank you note, as an item exclusively for your VIP clients.

Summary

So now you're clear on what Promotional Product Marketing is, and have got the mindset of approaching it as an investment in a campaign. Your campaign will help achieve one or more clear specific business objectives. You've stopped thinking about Promotional Products as a cost to be avoided or minimized.

Unlike many other forms of advertising, it's physical, it's got long-lasting impact, it's easily targeted, it's a great value for money, and super-flexible.

If you'd like to see more about the numbers behind these claims, register at www.getyournameoncoolstuff.com for the bonuses that come with the book, and download the "Facts and Figures" white paper from the Membership page.

Practical Exercise

Now take a moment to think about where, right now, you could do with some help – what's the most pressing need for your business?

Looking to get your existing clients to spend more with you?

Want to attract and retain your staff more effectively?

Aiming to reconnect with old contacts?

Take five minutes out from reading right now, go to the back of the book, or grab a piece of paper and write down the THREE most important things you need to achieve in your business or department over the next six to twelve months.

The most important things I need to achieve in the next 6-12 months are:

1).....................

2).....................

3).....................

Keep these in mind as we move to the next chapter and talk more specifically about campaigns and promotions.

Let's get Busy!

Making sense so far?

Want to watch a quick video which helps to explain this some more?

As you know, this book is interactive.

To get free updates and bonus videos, access to more resources, and upgrades to the book when new versions or editions are released, visit www.getyournameoncoolstuff.com

or scan this QR code

and follow the instructions.

CHAPTER TWO

Great Ways To Use Promotional Product Marketing For Your Business

I'm not against the whole MP3 download thing, and of course it's definitely very nice to have thousands of songs in your pocket, but the whole purchase experience is just different.

I'm old enough to remember what it was like buying an LP record as a teenager.

It was a whole experience, and a delight to the senses.

Allow me please a quick trip down Memory Lane…

When I was 16, a day's wages at my Saturday job would just about cover the price of a new LP (translation = Long Playing Record). I remember the experience of going through all the records in the racks in the shop, lifting them out to look at the sleeve, and reading the notes on the back. It was even better if it was a gatefold sleeve, maybe more to see inside, looking at the cover art, and anticipating how the tracks were going to sound. Then a decision made, and to the counter to pay, getting the record back in its bag, kind of an awkward thin square shape to carry, but very distinctive.

That "Max Records" yellow carrier bag was a sign of cool in my hometown back in 1979 —you've got a new record, and you're letting everyone know. Then you'd have to take it out on the bus on the way home and read every word you could find over and over. Finally get home and put it on the record player, see the inner sleeve notes, and be completely absorbed in 20 minutes of music.

Sound
Sight
Touch
Smell

Then get up and turn it over to put on the B-side. Sometimes there were great cool features or unexpected extras - lyrics, or bonuses like the wall posters Pink Floyd gave out with The Dark Side of the Moon.

Things started to go downhill with cassettes, then CDs diminished the experience further, and now iTunes and downloads – yes we get the music, and we've all got thousands of songs in our pockets, but somehow it's not the same – the whole experience is definitely different. I'm so glad I kept all my albums!

The power of "real things" is immense – whether it's my 12" vinyl record collection or a lumpy parcel received in the post at work, or a calendar mousepad that you can use again and again as a screencleaner, people love to be entertained and distracted by Cool Stuff.

You could say the same for business these days too – because so much of what we do now at work is online or virtual, it's refreshing when our attention is diverted by something real.

The first steps in getting any marketing message across are to **interrupt** and **engage** –and Promotional Products are great at doing this.

In this chapter, I'm going to talk about how you can harness this type of interruption and engagement to help you achieve what you need for your organisation. We'll look at the sort of business objectives you can realistically achieve when you Get Your Name on Cool Stuff. I'll talk about how Promotional Product Marketing campaigns can help you convert leads into customers, move them through the buying cycle, and turn them into loyal clients who will increase your profits.

What's your campaign trying to achieve? (really?)

One thing that Promotional Product suppliers often find frustrating are small to medium-sized clients who come asking for help with the hazy objective of "just getting the name out there". They sometimes misguidedly call it "brand building".

Now, unless you're already an international brand and household name with huge market reach, you really don't need to reach the general public about your brand – and you'll waste your money if you do.

Who are you really trying to reach?

In the small and medium-sized enterprises (SME) world, for the most part, people buy from people with whom they are comfortable, so your focus really should be on connecting with real prospects who genuinely have the scope to become clients, finding ways to make them feel good about you, and trying to keep them feeling that way.

Make sure that your campaigns make it easy for people to react the way you want. Sure, it's fine to let them see your cool logo and fancy branding, but make sure you include a message which is targeted and relevant, and focus your spending on concrete objectives like getting new customers, building loyalty with your existing ones, and increasing your profits.

Identifying Qualified Leads

If you don't know your potential clients already, you will need them to metaphorically put their hands up to identify themselves. You will probably have some idea about where you can find them, so your initial objective would be to make sure that you are also present in these places, so that they can easily let you know they are interested. This would probably require some more general approaches to cast your net more widely – maybe social media and traditional advertising, flyers, direct mail, trade shows, networking, webinars, etc. – and people may need an incentive to hold their hands up. The good news is that once your leads have identified themselves, you can consider them as Qualified Leads – and then you can add them to your more personalised buying funnel or sales process.

Multiple contacts with your leads

Let's face it, it really is pretty unlikely that you will turn even a Qualified Lead into a new customer with just one contact, whether it's a phone call, an email, a Facebook post, a Facebook ad, a radio interview, or a podcast. Even just a single Promotional Product may not cut it on its own. It's more likely that the cumulative effect of repeated contact messages across a range of media over a period of time will lead to a build-up of confidence in a seller (personally or in their company). This series of contacts helps to turn a prospect from being unconvinced or uninterested into an enthusiastic consumer of whatever you have for sale. Each contact helps to build credibility, some with higher impact than others. You can use Promotional Products within your sequence as high impact contact points to build credibility or deliver key messages.

Promotional Products for Lead Generation

When getting leads to put their hands up for you, you can use Promotional Products:

- as an incentive to sign up for a mailing list – given in return for an email address when you meet a lead at your trade show booth.

- as a vehicle for passing on ways they can get in touch, or your contact information – see the URL on this pen we're giving you.
- to raise awareness of what you do and pique curiosity – a USB key product which directs the lead straight to your website with more information on your products and services.
- to let people try your products - a sample of what you make,
- as a way to get them to come to visit your store – maybe send out a branded keyfob with a key attached to 1,000 addresses in the local area – invite recipients to bring the key to see if theirs will open the safe in your store on the weekend!

The unit cost to you of the Products used for these objectives would typically be at the lower end, because you are working with larger numbers, and expecting only a small proportion to actually reach leads who will turn out to be qualified.

A good example would be the lower value items handed out from the trucks which make up the carnival-style "Caravane" at the head of the Tour de France cycle race – typically low cost, budget items (including product samples) thrown out at random into the crowd – successful items encourage and get further engagement with the recipients, the worst ones are just thrown away and forgotten.

If you'd like to see my more in-depth review of the Tour de France Caravane from 2013, register at www.getyournameoncoolstuff.com for the bonuses that come with the book, and download the "Tour De France" report from the Membership page.

Turning Leads into Clients

In a small self-contained market like a specialist industry or in a commercial context where there is an easily identifiable number of players (maybe you can find them easily through online directories), you might already know who your potential clients are. If so, then you can start straight away with Turning Leads into Clients. This means it's up to you to make contact with them effectively, and then to find ways they can engage with you and enter into your buying funnel or sales process. This could involve outbound email nurturing programmes, content marketing and privileged access to blogs and information products, personal phone calls, lumpy mail, social media group memberships, sales rep visits, seminars, and events…

Using Promotional Products for Client Conversion

When you are looking to turn Leads into Clients, there's definite scope to use Promotional Products as a complementary element to your sales funnel.

Promotional Products are physical credibility builders for your brand, so use them to interrupt and engage with your Leads during the sales process in some of the following ways:

- As a thank you for spending time with you at a meeting – a decent quality pen (maybe printed with your contact name and URL?) makes a stronger impression as a meeting "leave-behind" than a business card alone.
- As a warm-up gift sent in the post as lumpy mail before an introductory phone call – this turns a cold call into a warm call.
- As an incentive to attend an event you might offer a free gift to the first 50 to enrol - you want to make sure people will come along to hear what you have to say.
- As a reminder of a seminar or event your prospect attended where they got some great content value from you – a notebook or portfolio, or sticky notes, which you encourage people to take away (and keep on their desks or by the phone at home).

Let's look a little more closely into some strategies for turning identified leads into clients.

The Membership Group Approach

This one, which can work for a company which wants to build a relationship with a number of key influencers and decision-makers in a new geographical area or a new client sector is about taking defined targeted leads and working on them to bring them into your customer funnel. It's like inviting people to be part of a membership group - and in fact, that is an exact tactic you can use.

A company I know did this successfully - their methodology was to invite thought-leaders and influencers who they wanted to attract as clients to be a part of a Mastermind group. They sent out a hard copy of a best-selling book on leadership by a well-known author to each of the target leads, along with an invitation to a lunch and a discussion session set around three weeks in the future, to be run by an accredited facilitator. People read the book (or at least skimmed it!), joined the lunch, and enjoyed the talk. As a result, they started to take the company which had organized it more seriously. Further lunches and sessions were scheduled for future months, and the programme continued. There was no attempt at any type of sale at all for the company's services, but they steadily built credibility, and naturally opened the door to more specific business opportunities. Not all the members of the Mastermind group became clients, but enough of them did to justify the investment in the programme.

In this example, the "Cool Stuff" we're talking about here (the Book) did not have "Your Name" on it – the promotional product (that Book) was free of corporate branding. However, the overall experience for the recipient was corporate-branded – which meant that the gift was linked to the company in the recipient's mind. The envelope, the accompanying letter, and the bookmark inside the book, as well the experience of the meal and the discussion session, all these things incorporated visual elements and branding, like the company's logo and URL, to ensure association.

This particular approach is not for everyone – it typically suits companies who are looking for a relatively small number of very high-spending clients and have the personnel, the budget, and the resources to be comfortable with spending time on slow-burn face-to-face relationship building. Following this exact way of working does imply a high cost investment per lead – but as with all marketing actions, if the value of a contract or business deal you stand to get from one converted lead is high enough, then the investment is justifiable.

Other Approaches for Conversion

You might consider alternative approaches on different budget levels, depending on the type of Lead you are looking to convert and how you want them to work with you in the future – face-to-face long-term contract / occasional purchases / online only - and adopt an approach which fits best with your business model.

Alternative 1) rather than sending a commercially available book, you can send your leads a more budget gift in the post –and include an invitation for them to join you at a drinks reception "meetup" at your shop / office / a local hotel.

Alternative 2) you email your targeted leads a link to a video on your area of expertise and invite them to subscribe or just to reply to receive a free gift - and to attend a live webinar on a relevant topic (make sure you arrange to send them the recording of it too in case they miss it or the timing is not suitable).

Alternative 3) you email your targeted leads an introductory chapter or two of your own book as an introduction ,and then invite them to subscribe to get a PDF version of the complete product and free updates as you add content and revise.

Alternative 4) - this is a tactic for identifying qualified leads - you use Pay Per Click ads on Google or Facebook ads to drive traffic to a free offer of a useful information product which you have authored – and when they sign up to get this, you can start to build a relationship through a pre-programmed series of email contacts.

Actually, you might find that more than one of these strategies works for different areas of your business, so don't automatically discount any of them.

Repeat Business – the value of better customer loyalty

It's a proven truth that repeat business costs a lot less to secure than new business, so it's genuinely worthwhile putting extra effort into making sure that your customers keep coming back to buy more from you. Turning a one-time buyer into a returning client is almost a science in itself, and you need strategies and tactics to make this happen for your business whatever it is. For existing clients who have already bought your products and services, your marketing priorities will be more about maintenance of that contact, building the goodwill so they will want to work with you again, having them refer you to their friends and colleagues, and making sure that they continue to think of you as the go-to resource for whatever it is you do.

Sometimes this area overlaps in real time with "Acquiring New Customers". For example, if you are running a booth at a trade show, you'll probably be meeting unknown potential clients, as well as some old friends who already work with you. Don't let this confuse your approach – you need a two-level strategy in this case. For the leads you don't know, you'll need to offer a simple lower value item with a more directly promotional message to attract and inform them. Maybe this item will also prompt some initial interaction to help you qualify the lead right there – and allow you to collect an email or phone contact from the ones you'd like to work with in future.

For those existing clients you will meet at the same show, your gift will be more about building loyalty – so an item that reflects their client status and helps cement your relationship would be more appropriate and more effective. For this, your gift might well be higher value, the branding would probably be more discreet, and the text or accompanying message would be less overtly promotional.

Building buyer confidence with Brand Maintenance

Very large companies often view global brand maintenance as a loyalty-building activity – though some of these may be beyond the scope of many readers here. Sponsorship of high profile sports such as Premier League football, or Formula1 motor racing, or global advertising campaigns, do play a part in helping larger companies dominate markets or hold onto their market shares. To do this takes deep pockets and a lot of patience; though it does work (otherwise they would not persist). If you are considering working with or buying from a certain brand, then whenever and wherever you see their brand name, it somehow does make you feel a little more comfortable about them. And when you see the name and logo of a company, a product, or a brand you already buy somewhere out of context, maybe on a roadside hoarding, or on the baggage trolleys at your airport arrivals lounge, something similar happens. You experience a gentle positive boost, and you're slightly comforted and reassured to see it, assuming of course your personal experience of that brand continues to be good. It's almost an endorsement of your own decision to work with that supplier.

Advertising activities like this build reassurance with existing clients, and a confident client is likely to be more loyal to your brand. If your client feels at home with your logo, then they probably feel completely at home with everything else about you too.

Smaller-Scale Targeted Brand Maintenance

This sort of large-scale action might be outside of your scope - but you can make similar things happen for your own brand in a more modest way using Promotional Products. You just need to target your campaign accurately on your existing clients – and make sure that you associate your name and logo with something which resonates and they can use in their normal day-to-day lives – Promotional Products are ideal for highly targeted work, and there's bound to be something out there with the product profile which will fit your objectives and suit your clients. Remember, if a client sees and uses your item regularly – and feels comfortable having it around as part of their life - then you are building genuine loyalty.

You can do it in a number of ways. Here are a few examples of campaign types with initial suggestions about the types of product which might work well in each case – though, as we'll see in the next chapter, actually making your final product choice is a little more involved. Please note, this is not a definitive list, and some products could certainly work well in more than one category.

- *Simple thank-yous* – headgear and apparel, leather gifts, speaker gifts, travel bags, travel adaptors, trophies, umbrellas, powerbanks, swiss multitools, wine, and wine-related gifts – unexpected or random thank you gifts can have a huge impact.
- *Ways to pass on new information or keep in touch* - Sticky notes, (each one printed with the new information you're sharing - or images of a new product), USBs (containing pdf brochures, pictures, videos), and fridge magnets (with new contact details or product info).
- *Keeping your name top-of-mind* every day gifts for use at home or at the office (especially for clients who buy occasionally) - pens, desktop items, calendars, pens, mugs, travel coffee flasks, notebooks, and stress toys.

- *Letting your clients have fun or make some noise in a crowd* (and be seen endorsing you) – clapper fans, bambam sticks, temporary tattoos, balloons, inflatables, stickers, wristbands, and button badges.
- *Showing affiliation and build a community* – membership badges, tieclips, brooches, cufflinks, phone covers, wristbands, and welcome packs.
- *Over-delivering or adding a free extra* – this is when you include an unexpected and unannounced free souvenir extra with your product when you make a sale – e.g., You sell jewellery? Your client gift is a polishing cloth. You rent cars? Your client gift is a cool keyring. You sell beer? Your client gift is a pack of playing cards.

Good quality interactions – with a long-term perspective

Building loyalty is an ongoing and constant process, not just a once or twice effort. A planned sequence of valuable contact actions or messages helps to keep your loyalty-building programme on track. There are ways to automate this, but you can also do it manually.

You do need to have genuine valid reasons for keeping in touch, such as sharing some product recommendations or how-to information, or other general information. Otherwise, there is a risk you will come across as insincere. When you give someone a promotional gift, hardly anyone will reject it or resent it, but you might not be able to afford to use a promotional product for every contact action every time in your sequence. Because people's responses to different types of messages vary, it's also useful to have variety in your approach, so it's good to make other types of contact too. Depending on your business process, this could be by phone, by email, or maybe in person. Make sure those contacts are also value-rich; think about "What's in it for me?" from your client's perspective. If your contact actions are repetitive and bring little or no value to the recipient, then you risk becoming a pest, and they'll get fed up with you quite quickly.

Work to build a reputation for great quality and content in all your communications when you're building loyalty – and of course, make sure that all the promotional items you distribute as steps in that process are great quality too.

Campaigns to generate Increased Profits

You can use conventional advertising to try to trigger specific responses from existing clients to help you build profits, and you can use Promotional Products too.

Any campaign which helps you increase overall turnover or average existing client spending should lead you to improved profits (assuming that you have your business set up to handle additional business efficiently and cost-effectively).

Campaigns like this work on the basis of reciprocity – you encourage your clients to spend more on your standard product offerings, and in return they receive a free gift.

Examples of specific Gift With Purchase (GWP) campaigns to promote sales and hence increase profits include :-

- Getting clients to upgrade to a more premium service or to buy a new product in your range.
- Encouraging clients to buy more per order, or to buy more often.
- Making clients aware of special offers.
- Offering limited edition "collectible" items as an incentive gift
- GWPs for early adopters of your new service or product.

- Online retailers offering incentive gifts for increased spending more per visit – online – e.g "Spend more than $149 today, and get a free hat'".

Merchandising - Selling your branded products

Merchandising is another way to increase profits using Promotional Products – the key difference here is that you are actually selling the products to your clients instead of gifting them. Rather than incentivizing purchases of your normal basic product range with a free gift, you're actually offering additional products for sale.

For example, the basic saleable product of a sports team is an admission ticket to watch a game. However souvenirs or club memorabilia, and other products bearing the club name account for huge additional revenue and profit potential. It's not just for the big players - souvenir product ranges at Club shops, whether members clubs and societies, or golf clubs and other sports clubs are a typical example of this seen in every town.

Merchandising is a long-established phenomenon, not only with teams and clubs, but also at tourist attractions like museums, galleries, etc. You can also buy branded merchandise related to films, festivals, theatre shows, carnivals, exhibitions, etc. In the music scene, concert tour merchandise has been a well-established feature for years - and now there are more examples of other media phenomena becoming events and going "on the road" - TV shows like BBC's Top Gear have transformed themselves into arena shows, and Harry Potter has a touring exhibition – all these shows charge admission of course, but they make more money selling related souvenirs too.

Merchandising for your company too?

Merchandising is not exclusively for the big names - if you have an active client base and enthusiastic supporters, it's worth considering if you can add a new revenue stream by selling branded merchandise in the form of souvenirs of your business too.

It's easiest perhaps for existing retailers who can simply add further branded merchandise lines to their standard products – e.g., you might operate a successful micro-brewery and sell through your own retail outlet. If at the same time you can also sell related products with your name on– for example branded baseball caps / barbecue aprons / can coolers, etc., this is great. Not only do your fans pay to drink your product, when they buy those other products they are paying you to advertise to their own friends and family.

It's a simple add-on to start selling merchandise if you already have a physical store, but if you don't have a retail outlet, don't be put off. You can easily add a webstore to your online presence.

Working on the Inside

The effects of Promotional Product Marketing are not restricted to external situations - better profits can also come from having a more switched-on, dedicated, loyal, and motivated workforce.

There are many situations where you can use Promotional Product Marketing within your company to help build a more positive internal environment. With more motivated salespeople, you should expect to see increased sales figures - but even without this, happier staff should give you better profitability thanks to more efficient operations (because of reduced staff turnover, lower absenteeism, and a more positive and collaborative work ethic).

Gifts for customers or gifts for staff?

I once knew a CEO who reacted with uncharacteristic fury when he heard that people were taking corporate gifts from the marketing store cupboard to give to the company staff in overseas offices they were going to meet on an upcoming overseas trip. His attitude could be summed up as "Gifts are intended for customers, as a thank you for what they buy from us. They're not for our own people. They already get paid well enough by us, so there's no need to give them presents as well – it's just a waste of money."

I felt this was an unusual and surprising reaction – surely the fact that people are pleased to receive and prepared to use their own company's gifts says something very positive about how they feel about their workplace? Obviously, we do hear of examples where people are getting into the marketing stock cupboard and selling items down at the pub, but I think that's relatively rare. Surely it's a good thing to have employees who are so comfortable with the company they work for that they are delighted to use a corporate gift, even if it was originally designed with customers in mind?

I know someone who was so down about the company she worked for that she absolutely refused to use or wear anything bearing the company name. She loathed that company so much that she even scratched the company logos of her office pens. But, if you are fortunate enough to have staff who love working for your company who like to wear company-branded clothes – or salespeople who like to use your company's branded hip-flask when they play golf with their Sunday mates - then I think you should capitalize on this and let them do it. This is free endorsement for your brand, your staff are clearly happy to be using these items, and these products are working harder for you than they would if they were still sitting in the store cupboard.

Staff Motivation

It would be unrealistic to believe that you can turn around a toxic workplace by just starting to give Promotional Products to your staff. On the other hand, if you already have the basics of a positive environment, using Promotional Products to further encourage positive behaviour, to raise awareness, to incentivise, to show gratitude for performance or attitude, or to publicise and promote new initiatives can help to make that workplace an even better place to be.

Some specific campaign ideas are here:

- Incentives for achieving sales targets
- Recognition of stellar performance for customer service or operations
- Apparel items for staff - either as a uniform or as casual wear
- New employee welcome packs
- Support materials for training and product knowledge
- Awareness of Wellness and Health programmes
- Long-service awards
- Annual performance awards
- Safety programmes
- Promotion of new company taglines or changes of focus
- Rewards for innovation
- Recruitment
- Christmas or New Year gifts
- Corporate retreats or conferences

Whatever the objective, there is a Promotional Product solution that can almost certainly help.

In summary, Promotional Product Marketing is more about the Promotion than the Product!

In this chapter, I've reviewed how Promotional Product Marketing can help with getting new customers – identifying leads and helping to turn these leads into clients. I've covered ways to build loyalty within your client base and some methods to increase profits through GWP and sales incentives as well as merchandising new own-branded products and internal gifts to enhance staff motivation.

Practical Exercise

Now take a moment to think about your own business situation, and look back at those three important objectives for the next six to twelve months you highlighted at the end of Chapter 1.

Think through the different objectives.

Are you clear about who you are trying to reach?

What you want to do when you "interrupt and engage" with your campaign?

Are you

- Identifying leads?
- Building a series of contact events?
- Converting leads you already know?
- Building loyalty?
- Maintaining your brand positioning?
- Selling more with GWP?
- Merchandising?
- Supporting an internal corporate message?

Take five minutes out from reading right now, go to the back of the book or grab a piece of paper and, referring back to the examples and suggestions in the chapter, write down some more details for your most pressing objective, describing

1   Who specifically does your campaign need to speak to?
2   Which tactics you will use?

Keep these in mind as we move to the next chapter and talk about Product choices

---

Let's get Busy!

Making sense so far?

There's more related material, ideas, examples, and worksheets on our Cool Stuff membership page.

Membership's free, and all you have to do to get access to the bonus materials including free updates to the Book is register now.

Visit www.getyournameoncoolstuff.com

or scan this QR code

and follow the instructions.

CHAPTER THREE

Choosing Your Products

Twenty years ago, a young British trainee manager got his first serious management job looking after a sales team handling his local UK market. Within a few weeks of his appointment, he received a mysterious package in the post – a classic lumpy parcel piece of direct mail marketing. When he opened it, he found it contained a calligraphy brush and Chinese ink, an unsolicited gift from an unfamiliar Asian airline. This guy didn't really know what to do with it – he knew nothing about Chinese culture, had no idea what the product was for, and no expectation of ever travelling anywhere outside Europe, let alone on that airline. He didn't bother to respond, and although the name Cathay Pacific seemed kind of exotic and interesting, he didn't really think too much more about it. In time, that gift moved off his desk, and ended up coming home - he showed his wife, and in the end it got shoved into a cupboard in their back room.

Fast forward now about 5 years, and the manager's job was changing in a very unexpected way – the company now needed him to fly to Hong Kong to carry out a research project in Asian markets. So guess which airline he chooses when presented with the choice of business class flights to Hong Kong - British Airways or Cathay Pacific? The memory of that mysterious and unexpected gift from a few years ago came back. He was familiar, of course, with British Airways from flying with them in Europe and they were perfectly fine, but why not try Cathay Pacific this time, seeing as how they were so kind as to send him that strange gift those few years ago?

That's the story of how I chose to become a Cathay Pacific customer. Since that first trip, I've flown with them well over half a million miles and because I now live in Hong Kong, they've really become my "home" airline. However, even if I had only just used them for that one trip, then I still reckon they would consider their promo product campaign five years previously to have been effective – the incremental value to an airline of even just one additional Business Class return fare from London to Hong Kong is far greater than the cost of a few cheap calligraphy sets.

So there's a promotional gift that worked like a timer ticking away in my subconscious for five years until the day came when I was ready to buy – and buy I did, without a moment's hesitation!

That's effective targeting, and great value for money!

In this chapter, I'm going to explain in more detail about practical product selection. I'll describe and look at a couple of traps you should avoid, and work through a three-step approach which lets you narrow down the choice to help you select a suitable product for your campaign.

1) Review your Campaign Characteristics
2) Define your Product Profile
3) Select your Connection Strategy

At the end, I'll also address two more common worries about product selection.

Look out for these traps! #1 - Window Shopping

When you're starting out, it's very easy to get hung up on which Promotional Product you are going to source. There's undoubtedly a great temptation to begin the process by looking through catalogues or searching online to find something which "looks good" or which just somehow stands out, and if you do start to browse online, you are quickly overwhelmed by a huge number of websites and online ads which just push product after product at you without a concern as to their appropriateness for your situation.

This is what I call the "window-shopping" approach, and whilst that can be fun as a leisure activity, or as way to spend Saturday afternoon with your significant other, it's really not an approach that will get the most from your time at work, or achieve your business objectives with speed and ease. There's a great tendency to get distracted and a risk that you will see bright shiny products in catalogues online which you happen to like personally - and then start working out ways to justify spending money to get them.

When you start out with this mindset, it's very easy to find yourself drifting away from the original purpose of selecting a promotional product – which of course is to pick something that fits the campaign objectives you are trying to achieve.

Be clear and disciplined about this- just as you would be about any other kind of advertising spending - and use your energy and time first to work out what you want to achieve.

Don't start out by jumping into selecting a product because you think it looks neat or because it seems like a cool idea.

Doing this is almost like going to see your doctor, and instead of having a 10 minute consultation, talking about your symptoms and the likely diagnosis and cure, you spend those 10 minutes entirely on your own in the pharmacy stock room, selecting drugs at random based on the colours of the packaging.

Trap #2 – "I like that, we want some too"

You might have been inspired by a particular gift you received from another company or something you saw in the shops – it might be a great product, but just because you *liked* it, doesn't necessarily mean that the same product is going to work as an *investment* to help *your* business. And if it's just not available for some reason, you're going to waste everyone's time in a fruitless search – when something more readily available would work perfectly well.

I've been dealing with a client who wants to get their name onto something – unfortunately it's clear that the poor guy I've been talking to doesn't really know how this fits into any type of marketing activity – his boss has just told him he wants some of these special design mugs so that they can give them out to clients. It's a special coffee mug which has a vacuum sucker on the bottom like a kid's arrow. It's available in retail, and been on TV, etc., etc. – and the idea is that it sticks firmly to a surface and is more difficult to knock over than a normal coffee mug.

I completely understand that this sucker makes the product stand out in some way as being different from other run-of-the mill coffee flasks, and it's undeniably a cool item. But if we look at the actual likely impact on their business, I'm not sure how this particular item would perform dramatically better for them than any other more standard, practical, and well-functioning mug.

Now if they were doing a promotion based on the stickiness of their services or products, or implying that their products are gravity-defying, or they have a message which relates to office safety or reliability - something along those lines which plays along with a theme - then they may have a point.

However, I really don't believe this is the situation this time.

My fear is that this is a case of someone senior in the organisation seeing something in a shop and thinking it would be cool to give this out to clients, and then instructing someone else to "make it so".

In this instance, the problem is that it's a new product, with trademark protection - and it is not yet available as a brandable corporate gift in reasonable quantities. We've actually been in touch with the manufacturers, and that's the situation.

We've told the client this, but they've decided they'd prefer to keep looking elsewhere in the hope that they might find exactly what they want.

Now for me, seeing as how this product is quite simply not available in the small quantity they will want (or at the price they will expect to pay!), it doesn't seem to make sense. The time and energy they will spend continuing to search for something as specific as this would almost certainly be better spent on talking with clients, or generating business in other ways.

What's more, if a "coffee flask" really is the right product to generate a positive financial response for them as part of a particular campaign they have in mind, then really any coffee flask will work, so long as it is properly functional, looks good, and its branding is appropriate. I don't believe that this particular fancy new flask which they have set their heart on is the only type of coffee flask capable of achieving their campaign objectives.

If they don't get this particular flask, it's very unlikely to undermine their campaign's success – and by delaying action on the campaign, they are opening themselves up to the opportunity cost of missing out on sales they could have generated if they had taken action earlier. My view on it is that they would be better off taking some (maybe imperfect) action now to test the effectiveness of the campaign. They could order 200 good quality, more conventional, and readily-available flasks that they can send out now, which would mean that they have something working for them on their client's desks right away.

A better way - follow this three-step approach

Step 1) Review your Campaign Objectives

Rather than starting with a pre-conceived idea about which product you are going to use, or searching through catalogues to give you an idea about something which "pops out", the right way to select a product is to start out first by being very clear about your desired outcomes - what you really want to happen.

Start with your ultimate objectives, and be clear about whom you are targeting, and what you want your campaign to achieve – then as you work out these answers, you see some of the issues and get closer to an idea of the sort of product which will work, you'll be able to define a Product Profile.

Step 2) Define your Product Profile

The questions you should consider about your Campaigns, and some of the typical answers I've heard before are below. I've also added a few comments and suggestions about how these help to define the product physical attributes or characteristics - the Product Profile - that would fit in each case.

What do you want to say?

"Buy another one"

"Please Subscribe"

"Tell me which you prefer"

"Thank you for your business, and please remember me next time you're buying widgets"

If you have a lot to say, and want to say it all on your product, then this will influence your product choice – not every product can be imprinted the same way, and different products have larger or smaller imprint areas or "advertising real estate" which you can use for your message. Pick a product with a large printable area – or else, if it doesn't have the space and you have plenty to say in your Call to Action, then consider using packaging, hangtags, or other printed-paper or card documentation to say it.

Remember that the style of the gift and the way it's decorated or presented will be influenced by many things, including where the recipient is in your buying process. If you are gifting to unknowns, your gift may well be more overtly promotional in its message. On the other hand, if all you're wanting to do is say "thank you", then you might want to be less obvious with your branding – when you're saying this to a client, your client definitely knows who you are, so a more subtle approach might be appropriate.

<u>Who you are going to say it to?</u>

The MD of your target company?

Their Office Manager?

A Secretary?

A sales guy?

Your own internal staff?

Your trade show visitors?

The general public?

Customers who already bought your top product?

The manager of a procurement department?

Put yourself in their position, and think about the sort of gifts that these people typically like or would expect to receive from someone like you – it needs be appropriate for their position and relationship to you.

This will help you rule out or include certain categories of item.

<u>What's your budget?</u>

"My boss tells me I can't spend more than USD5 on anything. But I don't know how many he wants"

"I don't know, give me some options"

If you don't have budget guidelines, then try to work out or ask someone how many items you need. Try to make an educated guess of some sort about this before talking to a supplier – this is likely to be one of the first questions they will ask. Consider how many people you need to give the product to. If it's for an event, how many are attending? Is this to cover needs for one event or for several? You could check how many you ordered last time – was it enough or too many? If all else fails and you can't get the answer from anyone, and you aren't in a position to decide yourself, then to get the ball rolling you can ask the supplier to suggest what would be a sensible practical volume to make it worth everyone's time.

There are many factors involved in setting a budget for a campaign, but if you're deciding the budget, consider the expectations of your recipients, and what the value of a successful campaign would be to your business. This will give you an idea as to whether you want to go with low, medium, or high budget items. Remember too that there is some connection between price and quantity availability - generally speaking, higher priced products are available in lower unit quantities than low price products.

There's more on calculating Return in Investment (ROI) of promotion product campaigns in Chapter 7.

How many units do you need?

One expression you'll become very familiar with is "Minimum Order Quantity" (MOQ). This is often a fairly flexible concept - some suppliers will tell you an MOQ based on what they would prefer to offer you, so if you are prepared to pay a little more per item, then they may be prepared to flex the volumes down. Remember, it takes your supplier and the factory just as long to handle and negotiate an order for 5,000 units as it does for them to handle and negotiate one for 50, so taking your small order on may cost them in terms of missed opportunities to take on other large orders. It is reasonable for your suppliers to ask for a higher unit price for smaller orders, and whilst it is always possible to negotiate, you shouldn't begrudge them this. Actually, because of the extra discussions and negotiations involved in handling unusually small orders, they can actually be more time-consuming for the supplier than a larger requirement.

Be upfront and precise about how many items you need with your supplier – they won't be able to give you an accurate price or delivery time without knowing what you are expecting. Also remember that you may have a different perception from your supplier - 100 items might seem "quite a lot, a good order!" to you, whereas your supplier might secretly consider this completely unattractive and a total waste of their time!

It's better to have these quantity discussions early on in the process. You are unlikely to get an enthusiastic or sympathetic reaction if your order turns from a big one to a small one at the last minute. Pricing is based on the quantity quoted, and different quantities attract different price points. You're in a much stronger negotiating position when you're talking about bigger quantities - but don't abuse it to get offered a "good" price and then expect to pay the same when you change it to a much smaller volume when you're ready to place your order. Your suppliers won't appreciate that, and may add salt to your quote the next time around.

For more guidelines on order quantity setting, see Chapter 5.

<u>Will just one item work, or do you need more than one?</u>

"To attract visitors to our trade show booth, we want a low cost mass market incentive e.g. 2,000 units below USD 0.50.

And then for people who are really interested when we get to meet them at the booth, we will need a smaller quantity of something really nice so they will remember us and talk to us later - we can spend up to USD15 on 100 units".

This response shows a clear understanding of the importance of having different products to help with different campaign objectives. Different categories of client or prospect may well respond best to different gifts. Promotional Products are certainly flexible, but if you systematically assume that you can use just one gift for all eventualities, you should probably think again.

<u>What are the crucial dates for your campaign execution and in your preparation process?</u>

"The seminar is in six weeks, and my boss is on holiday next week for a month. He needs to approve everything. Oh no! That means I need to get everything approved before Friday."

"The golf day is in four months, but with the public holidays coming up I'd like everything settled and ordered and delivered before the 15th next month."

"Our new product launch is in July, so we need to start our mailing campaign in June. That means receipt of the promo products end May. I understand it takes four weeks for production, so to be safe I should finally decide and place my order before mid March."

"It doesn't matter – as long as it takes is OK – these are for general use with our salespeople and there's no specific deadline."

This range of different typical responses reflects different levels of planning sophistication and different time pressures. Some products take longer to prepare than others, and whilst there is often a fast turnaround solution for standard products, the quality of the product or its decoration may not be as good as you would expect from normal production. Having a clear idea about your time frame is essential. If you don't have much time left, you'll probably have to make compromises on product choice – there will be some products that cannot be supplied in the time you have left.

Check on possible timing disconnects though. If your perfect product turns out to be a branded umbrella, and it's going to be ready for delivery just at the end of the rainy season, you'll have missed a trick. Likewise for hoodies, sweat shirts, and outerwear in those hot summer months. No-one's going to be thrilled to receive one of these!

<u>How long do you want this campaign to work for you?</u>

"It's to tell them about where our new shops are located right now."

"It's a long-term thank you gift - we want our clients to keep hold of it for the rest of their lives."

"It's to try to get them to sign up for this year's programme before government regulations coming in next spring mean we have to change it."

"It's to attract new leads to visit our booth this week – so it doesn't need to be super-long-lasting – but we need something really fast."

"It's to generate attention in the crowd during the sports event next month."

"It's a t-shirt to say thanks, so it needs to be durable, and something they'll be happy to wear for a few years."

"It's a t-shirt for the marshals at this year's race – it's not meant to be a souvenir. It's important that competitors can see them clearly - and they are instantly recognised as race officials. Also our main sponsor's logo must be clearly visible on any photographs. It's for on-the-day use only."

When you know these answers, you can have a better idea about the level of quality required. If you need your gift to only work for a short period of time, you can plan accordingly, ensuring that your gift is "value engineered" to suit its requirements. In other words, if you don't need your items to last for a long time, it might not always make sense to spend the money on top-of-the range-quality.

For example, do you really need to use genuine leather portfolios for an internal conference – perhaps good quality PU imitation leather products will work just as well for the time you expect them to be used, and still be appreciated by the recipients?;

You can value-engineer also with decoration techniques, because some are higher cost than others. Maybe there is no need to spend money on complex all-over printing techniques, or perhaps you can live with single-colour logo prints for once-only apparel? Or can you save some cash by using print rather than embroidery?

<u>How are you going to get it to your targets?</u>

"Brian will take them with him on the plane."

"The reps will just carry them in their briefcase."

"We'll just keep them in the stock room."

"We'll have a temp hand them out at the trade show."

"We'll just mail them out to everyone in one big blast."

Brian might need to check his baggage allowance, and should be prepared for questions with customs authorities when he arrives if duty is payable on imported items – especially if it's a big separate box of stuff.

Your reps won't thank you if the product you give them to use as leave behinds at client meetings are heavy or bulky.

The cupboard is not a distribution strategy! Products left in the stock room aren't promoting your company – there is a real risk they will just get forgotten. Can you assign someone who will be responsible for making these work, and for getting them handed out to the people they are intended for? Maybe make this part of your visitor routine - have the person who manages your meeting room bookings systematically check which gifts are required to be available for every meeting, and ensure that they are in the room in time for the meeting. Why not just add a checkbox on the booking form as a reminder?

For your tradeshow booth items, don't leave this to chance - will your temporary staff member know what to say to get the best value from the gift? You should identify and task someone responsible to train that person in what to do and say. Does this gift idea imply a need for any sort of packaging? If you need a bag for the gift, is there room in the booth to keep these and will people be happy to carry these around - think about portability and storage issues.

If you are mailing products out, check to see if they will fit in your company standard envelopes - if not, then you need to identify someone who is going to buy new envelopes. And you will need to define who's going to write the cover letter, who is going to print that cover letter and write / print the address - and work out your follow-up plan. Will you even be able to follow up personally on as many mail-outs as you intend for your campaign? Or perhaps it will be better to split the campaign into smaller batches and manage it over an extended time.

Defining your Product Profile – what next?

Working through these questions helps you define your Product Profile – once this is done, you will have a general idea of the scale and size of your ideal product, how many you need, some idea how much you can spend, and how long you're going to expect it to keep working for you - and how you're going to deliver it.

This immediately puts you in a stronger position to be able to communicate your needs to your Promotional Products supplier, however to narrow things down further, you should think about the Connection Strategy you're going to use to get your message across.

Step 3) Selecting your Connection Strategy

There are different ways to establish a mental connection between your product or services and your recipient. We base our product selection approach on four different Connection Strategies

1) Real Connection
2) Virtual Connection
3) Practical and Useful Connection
4) Personal Connection

You should select the one which fits closest with your business offering and the profile of your targeted recipients.

Real Connections

A Real Connection strategy is where your gift is a straight sample of what it is you make – food and drink are obvious ones. If you sell premium coffee blends, then a coffee sample would be a good call. If you're a cheese-maker, then vacuum-sealed selection packs might work well too.

It works for non-food products and services as well - if you make fountain pens, you're probably going to be ok if you stick with pens as your corporate gift. If you are in the business of selling financial advice, then how about a DVD of you speaking at a conference, or a USB containing spreadsheets and templates you're prepared to help with a DIY home finance review?

But even if you could give a sample of what you do or what you sell, you might not always want to do that - particularly with perishable items like food and drink, or with things that are consumed (and then easily forgotten).

If you're giving out perishable or consumable samples and you want the experience to last longer, consider complementary accompanying gifts (glasses / cutlery) or branded reusable packaging – wine bags / can coolers / biscuit tins.

Variants of this approach include where you give a sample of your product, but you present it in an unusual way. Perhaps you can incorporate your product into a paperweight? A basic unit of your product may be just too unmanageable to offer as a sample – things like steel, sand, concrete and other building materials, or commodity products like nickel - but maybe you can give a little piece of it somehow and build that into a truly unique Promotional Product.

This works well with commemoration or thank you gifts - I still have a desktop paperweight I've used for 25 years with a polished piece of metal rod embedded in it which commemorates the first cast from a new steel plant installed in Sheffield.

Another way forward to approach this is if your existing customers use your products in a downstream manufacturing process. Maybe you can work with one of those and use their products as your Promotional items? Again this is common in the steel industry – one company I worked for had a whole range of metal goods - hip flasks, pens, and card cases – all made from its own steel, and each with a little explanation paper insert to point this fact out to the recipients. Using Promotional Gifts like these showcases a little piece of what you do, and how well your product works for other people – and builds confidence that your product will work equally well for your prospect too.

Virtual Connections

The Virtual Connection approach is used when your own product is difficult to sample, or a real connection is impractical in some other way. It's not practical for banks to give out money – but related products like money clips, "something gold", or desktop calculators or piggy banks, can make a virtual connection to financial services providers, banks, and wealth management professionals.

Similarly, products that recall your product or service through their *form* - design or shape - can work too. We're all very good at perceiving meaning through an icon or a symbol, and a representation of the real thing can be a powerful tool – stress "squeezy" items shaped like your product or currency symbols (for financial services) or die-cut products such as sticky notes, shaped fridge magnets or silicone moulded USBs in the form of your product or your logo, or a related icon, are all good examples of how this strategy can work.

You can also use a product that in its *function* suggests a link to your product or the benefits you get from it. A training or consultancy provider could consider notebooks and pens, or an item that implies a link with learning or mental agility. You could use Rubik's cube products, or other types of puzzle items like tangrams or jigsaws.

Another type of virtual connection hinges on *location* – where will your client be when they need your service or product? If your client is likely to think of you or realise they need your services in the office, then office- based products will help them make that connection. If your customer will think of your product when they are in the kitchen or preparing a barbecue, maybe the fridge magnet, the corkscrew, or the apron would work better. If they think of you when they are driving, then you might want to consider static cling stickers, a windscreen sunshade, or a USB charging device that plugs into the dashboard power outlet.

Practical and Useful

Products that make a connection based on their practicality and usefulness for your target audience are also popular and successful. If you get it right, these are often the items that recipients will treasure and hold onto for years in regular use. There is strong appeal when an item fits these categories. The flipside is also true, so it pays to be careful - there's a risk of an equal measure of strong dislike if an item is perceived as being impractical and useless.

Usefulness is also a matter of taste and personal preference. Unless your intention is clearly to make a "fun" gift (see "Personal" below), items that don't have an obvious practical use for most people may be poorly received irrespective of how beautiful you might think they are. This can seriously undermine that positive impact you were looking to achieve. You might be surprised at how many well-intentioned gifts of local craft or artwork are left behind "accidentally on purpose" in conference hotel rooms – abandoned by attendees as being impractical to bring home, and with no obvious usefulness.

There are plenty of practical items to choose from, so select carefully from these general categories being mindful of your recipient's likely tastes and preferences, your own budget and, if applicable, the context where your own products and services fit most naturally.

Gifts like portfolios, notebooks, pens, powerbanks, chargers, travel adaptors, USBs, laptop bags, and screencleaners tend to fall into the "Office and Business" category. For "Family and Leisure" orientated products, consider umbrellas, sunglass pouches, backpacks, picnic baskets and rugs, drinkware, bottle coolers, drybags, in-car chargers, and multi-tools.

If you can make a virtual connection with your product and service too, whilst also delivering practicality and usefulness, this can only increase your gift's impact.

Personal Connections

If the other connection strategies don't seem to work for your campaign, or if you can't find a brandable product you are comfortable with which meets the requirements of your Product Profile, then try to find a way to connect to your prospect or client with something entertaining, attractive, or gently humorous. This can be difficult, because people have different views as to what qualifies, so of course it's a very subjective decision. If you stick with a middle ground, or with popular mainstream themes, this approach should work well most of the time.

For most businesses, everything "works" because of the people involved, and because of our personalities and the personal connections we can make. If you can appeal to people's emotions somehow – by finding a way to make them smile, or by appealing to their senses through attractive and eye-catching design, this really can build rapport.

Here's an example - if your target audience is unlikely to respond positively to a standard mid-range gift at your trade show booth, you might be better off trying a personal connection through an 'experience" approach. You can find ways to make this fun without costing a fortune. One simple example is to print a huge eye-catching (relevant!) tagline on a backdrop to your booth - and repeat the same line or image maybe on a simple "uniform" (this can be a few promotional t shirts) for your team to wear. Have a photographer take instant pictures of your visitors posing with the team. The visitors get to take their pictures home in a branded picture frame. The bonus for you is that they are effectively captive at your booth whilst they wait with you for the photo to "come out". So this give you a great opportunity to talk a little longer with them so you can ask qualifying questions and start to build rapport.

To summarise, after you have narrowed down the options by following these three steps

1) Review your Campaign Characteristics
2) Define your Product Profile
3) Select your Connection Strategy

You and your promotional products specialist will be in a much stronger position. From the hundreds of thousands of products available, you should now have a manageable shortlist. You can select with confidence from this list, knowing that each item will be a good fit.

Two Product Selection Worries - and what to do about them

Worry #1 - I'm worried my product will just get thrown away or passed onto the kids. How can I be sure people will like it?

Professional marketers often secretly worry that their carefully selected Promotional Product will be rejected - just thrown away or given away to somebody's children.

It's hard to guarantee that no-one will junk your product. We all have different ideas about what makes Cool Stuff. Whilst the steps we worked through previously will certainly help, in addition, it's worth thinking about the following ways to minimise the risk.

Quality and distinctiveness

None of us really have space in our lives for poor quality non-functioning branded promotional products. So any product you give out needs to be at least as good as what is generally available on the market at a "good" quality level.

Quality – does it feel ok?

In this context, I'm referring to "subjective quality", so if you'd like to read more about the "conformance to Spec" quality issues, register at www.getyournameoncoolstuff.com for the bonuses that come with the book, and download the "Specification Quality Issues" white paper from the Membership page.

Subjective quality is about perception and emotions - what people are thinking about and experiencing when they say "oh I like that, it looks and feels like a quality product". It includes elements of practical functionality, and how the product feels when you hold it in your hand, its build, aesthetics, and design

It's about your own confidence in the product too – and how you think people will react to it.

This means for a pen that you need to have the confidence that it actually works properly as you would expect from, well, a pen! It writes ok without scratching, it doesn't break apart when you press it on the paper to write, and the ink flows smoothly. In practice, there is nothing more disappointing than a product that promises, yet fails to deliver. And it reflects directly on your brand if it's your name on that product. The first person your client will curse when your pen leaks in their pocket will be you - not the pen manufacturer (they don't know who that is!)

These things can be rather subjective, yet even more so are ideas about how you like the way it looks, the noise it makes when it clicks or twists to open, and how that mechanism feels, the gloss of the printing, the colour palette, etc., and what "impression of quality" do these things give you about the product.

If you personally feel positive about these aspects, there's a reasonable chance your recipients will do too. If you are genuinely uncertain, then that feeling could well be shared, and that item is probably best avoided.

Get a wider view though – try to get "buy-in" from friends and colleagues – ask your supplier for working samples. You don't need them to have your brand name or logo imprinted on them at this point in time, you just want a "random" sample from a previous order for another of your supplier's clients, which lets you see the quality and how well it works. Set up an informal focus group and run some tests in the office to get feedback so you can see how people react.

In reality, you will know poor quality products when you see them. Review samples of the product you are planning to buy, and satisfy yourself and your peers that it works at least as well as typical commercially available industry standard products and that it feels and looks good.

Getting people to hold on to your gift

Basic functionality and decent quality will help to make sure that your gift doesn't go directly to the recycling bin on receipt – but assuming you've got over that hurdle, one of your campaign objectives might be for people to keep hold of it longer than the time it takes to respond to your Call to Action (CTA). To have them do this, you need to find some unique angle - a way that makes it distinctive.

We all have coffee mugs, and most people have one or more USBs at home or in their office drawer, and in truth, everyone's got more pens than they need already. So unless you are giving your prospects and clients a genuinely new product they don't already have, you'll be fighting for a space amongst their existing personal possessions. Your gift needs to be something pretty good to justify them displacing their old one with yours.

Consider variations of existing products that bring something new – an unusual and very cool design, or a higher spec version of a common product. Perhaps select a top grade leather mouse pad, rather than yet another generic rubber-backed fabric mat. Or consider multi-function items - a 2-in-1 charger and speaker, or a pen which doubles as a bottle-opener. You can also look for products with a twist that can be used in a different way or in a different place - a charger designed for in-car use, or a memory stick shaped like a credit-card so that you can easily keep it in your wallet.

Be on the lookout though for possible product disconnects – if you're a top quality brand using a product which looks cheap, then that's a disconnect you'd usually want to avoid. Cheap, standard-looking promotional products rarely appeal to high-end clients. Real "High Net Worth" individuals don't need and won't want cheap stuff, however cool they may seem to you - and they may be insulted if you try to press them onto them. For these contacts, you might want to work out a different, more personalised strategy using fewer, more expensive gifts – and perhaps restricting your branding to the bag and accompanying materials.

Passed-on Promos

"Thanks for the XXXX - my kids will love it."

If your heart sinks when you hear this, and you think your campaign's been a failure, think again – all may not be lost. Passed-on Promos are good news too.

Whilst you might think of your primary campaign target as the client or prospect who will spend money with you, Promotional Products still keep working even when they are passed on to someone else. New recipients will be pleased to get something unexpected, and may be intrigued and curious to know more about you - and the original recipients may also feel good about you because you've made them look good by putting them in a position where they can be "the giver".

Younger recipients of passed-on promos are also potential future clients – if your product is considered good enough to be kept around in their homes, then it will keep doing its job softly reminding your prospects of your brand.

And when this happens, you're creating a future generation of customers who grow up comfortable and familiar with your brand name at home - it worked for me with that pack of Aer Lingus playing cards.

Here's another example – a few years ago I took part in a dragon boat race at our home in Hong Kong. One of our team members worked for a UK bank, and they supplied the team with some standard T-shirts showing the bank's name and logo all over it. My children were about six, eight, and ten years old at the time, and they along with the other paddlers' children, were thrilled to get team shirts too.

Later that same year, we went for a holiday visit to England to visit family - the children spotted the logo and bank name from those shirts on buildings and hoardings in the High Street. They were really excited to be able to point it out and recognise it ,and thought it was cool that they'd had shirts with that logo too. They still remember the name of that bank 10 years on – that's a real personal connection.

So in fact, if your gifts do end up being passed on to your children or someone else's that's not necessarily a bad thing - you just might be starting to build a new generation of fans.

By the way, if you're actually thinking of giving out toys or gifts that you can reasonably expect will be passed on to or used by children, you should clarify this with your supplier. Take the steps necessary to find out what the appropriate product safety testing and disclaimers and notices are in this case, so that you ensure you comply with any requirements in the location where you plan to distribute your items. Talk to your supplier about what is required to reassure yourself that you are adequately covered. If there is some doubt, it might be better to rethink your plans rather than to take risks.

Worry #2 I'm worried that my products will go "out of date"

The first situation to consider is that of a product which is so old that its functionality is compromised – i.e. it has perished, dried up, gone rusty, decayed, gone sticky, or is otherwise no longer usable.

Talk to your suppliers in advance about this, and they can give you an indication as how long it would be prudent to store your particular item – in practice, most non-food items can last a year or so in good storage conditions – some products, as we've seen before, do last much longer when they are out in the market working for you! Note particularly with pens that it's good to keep the stock turning so that you don't risk the ink drying up.

If you do have to store items for any length of time, then pay attention to the condition of your storage areas – don't just leave Promotional Products in the garage or dumped on the floor in the back of the warehouse. Remember that this is high value advertising ammunition, and you need to keep it primed ready for use. Look out for damp, humidity, water ingress, excess heat, frost, or ice – any extreme is bad news for your Cool Stuff. Keep your products in a stable atmosphere, ideally indoors at comfortable room temperature and make sure that air is circulating. Nasty things can happen right under your nose – badges going rusty, glue coming unstuck (on books, portfolios), imprint inks getting sticky, or water staining. Be mindful of these risks, and store your products appropriately.

And rotate your stock – use the old ones up (or give them away) if your reorder arrives before you've finished using the previous batch.

The second "out of date" situation is when the product still works fine, but it was designed to be time-specific and that date has long-since passed – e.g. it's got "2013 - The Gathering of the Wise Ones - Convention 2013" printed all over it.

Unique date-specific gifts that name-check or otherwise identify a single occasion along with your brand or other message can be good. If it's a memorable event and people were proud to attend, and they will be comfortable continuing to advertise (and endorse) your brand by wearing that shirt, or carrying that backpack, then you will get good value from the gift.

If it's not so high profile, and for some reason people might feel less comfortable wearing your event details emblazoned across their chest, then the longer term branding impact and value you get from the gift will be reduced. In this case. it would be better to be more discreet. Be realistic about how the general public see your business and might interpret your messages and taglines!

If you do decide that you will put a date on the products you use – and don't get me wrong, this really is a great strategy for some events if you've got enough potential recipients to make it worth your time and effort to place a specific order - then make sure you don't over-order and end up with a cupboard full of products no-one's comfortable gifting after the event.

Here's one idea if you're creating a formal seminar type event and want to offer a gift your delegates will take home and use afterwards. A good quality PU Leather portfolio or compendium product could work well or maybe a backpack or a satchel bag. You might be tempted to print the name of the conference and the dates of the event on the product – that can be ok, but in three or four year's time it is going to look really quite out of date. If you can be sure it will last a lot longer, then maybe in 10 to 15 years time it will have some "vintage" value, but there's still strong risk that people will be tempted to throw it away in a year or two to move on to something less obviously "old".

One way to avoid this is to make the date-specific element of your gift a temporary feature which can be removed. You can do this by ensuring that there's a small window insert for business cards inside the portfolio, or something similar on the bag. Just arrange to print a small order of cards – business card size –including text and comments and the date relating to your event - ideally along with a CTA and an offer.

Insert one card into each window – any products not used at the event can have the cards removed later and put back into stock for personalising for your next event when you print up the next set of cards.

This gives you the convenience of being able to select one product for a series of multiple events on different occasions, maybe even with different titles and themes – but you still benefit from economies of scale on your order for the Promotional Product. Your supplier can probably also help with the card design and printing too, so that shouldn't be extra pressure on your time.

There's a simple way to make sure you don't fall foul of either situation – just be careful on quantities to avoid buying products you can't usefully consume in a reasonable period. It might be tempting to try to save a few cents per unit by upping your order, but it's often a false economy. Just don't buy too much!

In Summary

So now you know not to go rushing headlong into choosing a product or wasting time window-shopping or blindly following a whim or inspiration from someone else's great idea. You can work through the three-step approach to define your ideal Product Profile, and select from the different approaches for your Connection strategy. Not only this, you can take the steps to make sure that your product will be appreciated by your recipients - and you'll be mindful of what to do to stop your products going out of date.

Practical Exercise

Take five minutes out from reading right now, go to the back of the book or grab a piece of paper and review that most pressing current objective you identified at the end of Chapter 2. Remind yourself of your campaign targets and the tactics you will use.

Now... start to build up your Product Profile by answering these questions from the chapter.

1) What do you want to say?
2) Who you are going to say it to?
3) What's your budget?
4) How many units do you need?
5) Will just one item work or do you need more than one?
6) What are the crucial dates for your campaign execution and in your preparation process?
7) How long do you want this campaign to work for you?
8) How are you going to get it to your targets?

Then decide on your Connection strategy – which of these works best for you, your targets, and your product offering?

1) Real Connection
2) Virtual Connection
3) Practical and Useful Connection
4) Personal Connection

Don't forget !!

This book is interactive – pick up access to free bonus materials, videos, audio materials. and checklists, when you register for your free membership.

visit www.getyournameoncoolstuff.com

or scan this QR code

and follow the instructions.

CHAPTER FOUR

Why You Need A Promotional Product Pro —
And How To Choose A Supply Partner

Back when I was working in France in the early '90s, there was a huge craze for corporate pin badges. Every company had at least one design, and people were starting to build collections. A UK-based supplier I knew had actually produced a pin badge in the past, but because no-one in the UK was really interested or liked them, they hadn't bought any more for ages. But they were fighting to get hold of items like this in France! Surprisingly, it was really hard work for the people in that company's French office to get their UK marketing department to take their request seriously and send more badges across to Paris. It took weeks and weeks before they arrived - by which time the moment had pretty much passed.

It's rare to find that a promotional product you already have is completely in line and in tune with a national craze in another country - the French guys found it really frustrating not to be able to take this further. And more than that, it was a golden opportunity missed to generate some great goodwill and positive feeling for that company's brand at that specific moment in time.

Another international company I knew had offices in China — their Beijing office once produced some decent quality notebooks — these were intended for local clients, as they included text written in Chinese to introduce the company and to talk about its product range.

The local clients liked them for sure, and what's more they were in huge demand internally too, for salespeople and office staff elsewhere in the company. They loved the fact that it was their company's branded product, but so different from the ones they could get in their own countries. With that intriguing and incomprehensible Chinese text, I think people enjoyed the exotic flavour of these books. There were lots of requests for a re-order when the first delivery had all been given out, but it never happened – I don't really know why.

This is another good example of how a product initially intended for clients in one market turned out to be a great fit in a different market. In this case, it could have been an effective internal ad for the company's China activities in other countries - a bit of internal marketing to gain internal organizational support and improve goodwill for that office could have been pretty useful.

Sometimes, you never know how successful your campaigns are going to be. If your customer-focused products turn out to be popular in other markets from the ones where they were initially targeted, be receptive, and if an opportunity likes this presents itself, then capitalize on it. Listen to what the people in your company are telling you and set things up so that you can be positively responsive.

Why you need a Promo Product Pro – and how to Choose a Supply Partner

If you dismiss Promotional Product Marketing as a low priority activity for your organisation, then that's how it will stay. When you underestimate the power of this form of marketing, you'll miss out on some good opportunities to attract new customers, build loyalty, and improve your profits.

Most senior marketing people don't normally spend much time thinking about Promotional Products – they have a lot of other responsibilities to cover and internal meetings, planning activities, events, and often a whole department to run too. A practical way to give it some priority is therefore to appoint someone (or appoint yourself!) as your firm's Promotional Product Pro – a "champion" for this type of marketing – with the remit of finding a way to make Promotional Product Marketing an easy, normal part of your regular marketing activity.

Allocate responsibility, and set things up in such a way that your firm's Promotional Product Pro really learns how to make Promotional Product Marketing work. That way, when there's an opportunity to do more with your marketing, then they're ready to step up.

This chapter and the two following are all about the "nuts and bolts" of your campaigns, and how your Promotional Product Pro can handle supplier selection, order placement, and the order management process better.

In this chapter, first I'm going to explain why it's worth your effort investing some time personally to make sure you've got a Promotional Product Pro working in your organisation. Then we'll turn the spotlight on suppliers – and how the Promotional Product Pro approaches the choice of who to work with.

Becoming a Promotional Product Pro

Being the go-to person who knows how to get Your Name on Cool Stuff is not only a good thing for your organisation, but it's also great for building that person's personal status and reputation in the organisation too. And if that person's not going to be you, then pass this book on (after you've read it) to the person who will do it. Or you can get a free PDF version of the book to pass on when you register for the bonuses here! www.getyournameoncoolstuff.com

Who looks after Promotional Products in your company?

You'd be surprised how many people I meet who really hesitate to get involved, or are reluctant to put themselves forward to handle the actual sourcing of promotional products – sure, dealing with suppliers and factories might be way outside your normal day-to-day job scope, but with practice and some insider knowledge (and maybe some outside help from a decent Promotional Products Expert who can do some of that heavy lifting for you and will work on your behalf to make sure everything goes to plan), it's not difficult to get good results.

A practice I see a lot is that sourcing promotional products is "delegated" to the most junior staff in the office. Sometimes, this can work pretty well if the job has really been properly delegated - in other words, a clearly defined task, along with the responsibility and authority to make it happen, is given to someone capable of handling it - but not every manager is a good delegator.

Very often, the situation is that a very junior person is instructed to "just get some giveaways" by someone very much more senior, and they are left to somehow get on with the job without any knowledge of the purpose, the quantity required, the message the campaign is intended to send, the timeframe or even the budget – and almost certainly no real idea of how to actually manage the process.

Doing this is plain bad practice, wastes everyone else's time, and gives a bad impression of your firm to outsiders. You probably wouldn't assign a junior staff member to "arrange some advertising in the newspaper" or "just write a white paper to include on some emails and send them out to our clients" without clear guidance, so why would you think it's OK to do the same with a Promotional Product Marketing initiative?

Delegation – but not really

When people do this, the result of course is an inevitable and endless circling-back to "ask the partners" or "see what my manager thinks", with a disproportionate amount of delay and wasted time spent selecting and rejecting products. Of course, virtually no time is spent on working out a plan for a real campaign that can generate results. It often ends in stalemate, frustration, or "in the end we decided not to bother because we ran out of time" or a rushed attempt to produce a decidedly second-best item ("something, *anything*! What can you do?") delivered at the last minute – and unlikely to meet any sort of campaign objectives other than the feeble and often pointless "just getting our name out there".

Disappointing results from this experience then reinforce management feelings that this is all too difficult and not worthwhile - and staff feel unenthused and reluctant to get involved in future campaigns or to respond positively to future requests for help if opportunities arise to do more of this. Time to break the cycle of negativity!

Action takers - you can help your company do it better

If you recognise yourself in any of these situations – either as

1) the reluctant marketer,
2) the boss or
3) the hapless staff member –

it's time to change things around, and get

1) properly stuck in,
2) give a bit more direction, or
3) try to find a way to get more guidelines, and take some initiatives yourself.

Becoming a Promotional Product Pro – What's in it for me?

If you're a marketing professional taking the time to read this book and looking to learn something new, this is a chance for you to build your own expertise. When you get pretty good at working with Promotional Products to achieve your company's objectives, you'll start to see the benefits of that on a personal level too.

It can certainly happen that on occasion you feel like there's some sort of obligation to provide a gift at an event. So when that happens, take it as an opportunity to turn this into a positive - think a little out of the box, and turn things around.

Remember the hard value of a promotion for you is what you get back from it – is there something you can do in this upcoming situation to turn this from an expense line item into an investment that pays?

Sure there's probably some extra work involved, but there' a real upside to making a success of this. If you can create an unexpected buzz with what you do, or differentiate your company from the crowd in a good way, or gather the contact details for a whole bunch of interesting people who you've also prequalified as having some interest in what you do or what you say, then you're well on the way to getting measurable success from your campaigns.

When you're the Promotional Products Pro in your organisation you'll get praise and thanks for doing a great job - and colleagues and managers will see you as the "go-to" person with a great track record of getting products for your firm which arrive on spec, on time, all looking good, and which meet the campaign objectives. That improves your own standing in the organisation, and of course, it's something you can take with you to your next job - or use for yourself when you're running your own business.

The Promotional Pro's approach to selecting a supplier

Choosing the right supplier is crucial. A supplier holds many of the keys which will make or break your campaign, so it's worth investing time and effort to get the right one. You can choose to manage the process independently, working directly with a factory or through an online provider, or you can partner with a Promotional Products industry adviser, who can work with you to manage this – and do a lot of the "heavy lifting" for you.

Your Experience

You might have plenty of experience sourcing products from factories, and plenty of resources to throw at this — companies who are experienced at retailing and sourcing products for their own core business might feel that it's a straightforward add-on to their current operations to source extra items to use for a promotional campaign or as "GWP" (Gifts with Purchase).

Even some companies which specialise in other activities may have sufficient resources to allow their staff the time and freedom to do Promotional Product research for themselves, and to work directly with web-based providers or directly with producing factories, successfully making all the arrangements themselves.

Getting some help

However, not everyone has these resources available, and there are also just as many who do have the resources, but prefer to subcontract this work and get some help.

We don't all try to be completely self-sufficient and do everything ourselves at home. For example, most of us hire plumbers, painters and builders for those specialist jobs we don't have the time or expertise to handle ourselves, and even though we might do a bit of gardening for fun, we probably also buy some food from the supermarket rather than manage our own smallholdings. So it makes sense to take the same approach at work – there's no need to try to do absolutely everything ourselves there either.

Today, even larger companies who have their own procurement offices are increasingly comfortable about outsourcing Promotional Product supply. For sure, they can manage the campaign and product design and plan the objectives, and handle the mechanics of delivery to their target base – but even though theoretically they could also handle much of the sourcing work too, many prefer to pass on the actual sourcing responsibility to experienced third party specialist Promotional Product companies who can handle the nuts and bolts of the sourcing process for them.

Working with someone who thinks like you do

Whichever route you go with, when you're choosing a supplier, look for early signs which can give you an impression of how it will be to work with them – try making some initial contact and look out for the ones who you find it easy to communicate with, the ones who get your ideas and who you feel comfortable talking to. Don't be fooled into thinking that this is a real simple operation – you're about to get involved in a potentially complex manufacturing process with a lot of moving parts. To get it right, there will need to be a lot of interaction, so make sure you're comfortable with your partners!

Most people prefer to deal with companies who share a similar approach to their own, and they're most comfortable working with people who understand their own marketing challenges. At Synco Marketing, my company in Hong Kong, we tend to focus on working with professional services companies. We have other clients in many other areas too, of course, but we've developed a business approach that's designed to have a particular style which complements that of our key client base, and this gives them a degree of reassurance and comfort. And of course they are busy people under pressure to perform, which means that they are willing to pay a fair price for great products and great service.

At Synco Marketing, we're lucky enough to deal with quite a lot of Promotional Product Pros in our client companies. They really know their stuff, completely get the concept of how to run a campaign, are clear on their objectives, and are mindful of how to measure the response. They don't want to deal with factories or suppliers themselves and spend time haggling over irrelevant product details. We love dealing with clients like this - it makes life easy for them and us.

Finding suppliers online

A Google search for any type of product and the word "promotional" will give you millions of choices. You'll come up with lists of traders, agents, and factories, as well as people who are one-product specialists - if you've got the patience to work through them – even the first two or three pages, then I wish you well and every success. I know I don't have it, and I'm an industry insider who spends every working hour in my business thinking about Promotional Products.

Dealing Direct – buying straight from a factory

This might seem tempting, and many of our clients have looked at Alibaba and similar sites for all sorts of products. They've tried to contact a factory direct – not surprising really, a lot of people do think this is a cheap way to get stuff. It's absolutely true that directory sites like this *are* a useful resource for full-time purchasing professionals and *yes*, you can find information about lots of factories who say they can make the product you want. However, unless you do this all day every day, we recommend *caution* for *lots* of reasons.

In most cases, you will find that the majority will only want to sell in huge quantities to European and American distributors, and are not at all willing and able to deal with individual enquiries from corporate buyers or the general public. For those that make it look as though they are more open, in spite of the promising-looking entries and "chat now" boxes in those directories, it can be pretty difficult to make personal contact successfully.

And even if you do make some contact – who's actually going to be looking after your business? Can you be confident that the person you end up with really understands what your expectations and requirements are? Do you think they will be willing and able to send you a physical random sample so you can check to see that the product really does look like its picture, when you're only in the market for 250 pens?

Your friendly factory contact

I'm making generalizations here, but this is borne out by years of experience of talking with factory sales people. The people who work in sales departments in factories are often very good at their job, but let's be clear about that, there is a possible mismatch here with what you want.

Being good at the job – for your factory contact – means they are good at selling to maximise the production capacity of their own factory. This means they can give you the price of things their factory makes, and can tell you how long it normally takes to deliver their normal production. But it also means that they might feel it's ok for them to bump your comparatively small order back a few weeks in the production schedule if they get a huge order from a U.S.-based retailer a couple of days after they accepted yours.

Remember also that they aren't experienced Marketing Professionals.

This means they will be **unable** to:-

1) Advise you on the suitability of their products for your situation.
2) Propose other product alternatives which might work better for you.
3) Recommend ways to leverage your campaign or design for maximum impact.
4) Help you develop a Campaign which will help to improve your business.
5) Make sure your selected product fits with other items (from other factories) which you might need at the same time.

I'd strongly recommend that you steer clear of any direct factory contacts, or any other single-product specialist, as they are unlikely to be in a position to give you the range of advice and support you really need.

If you do go with it, then there is a good chance you'll end up spending a lot of time sorting out problems yourself. Trust me when I tell you that this is a painful way to buy.

Multi-Product promotional product websites

Along with factories, you might find a lot of these promotional product "catalogue" sites popping up on your Google search.

Whilst these might be pretty good for giving you product ideas and checking out variations on a theme, e.g., different-shaped coffee mugs – it's entirely possible to waste hours searching through *thousands* of options until you find a product you like.

It's easy to get sucked in, with enticing search functions and other bells and whistles, and holding your attention is just what these sites are designed to do. But once you've found a product you like, be prepared for surprises. Remember you are buying bespoke decorated items, so it's really not quite as straightforward as buying a book from Amazon!

You might also ultimately discover that the supplier won't send products to your location. (Note that this does seem quite common, particularly if you have an Asia Pacific region address).

Also whilst these sites may give you someone to "talk to", if you're not in the same time zone, it might be hard to get someone on the phone. And if you do reach someone, do you think their salespeople can really have personal experience of *all* those thousands of products they advertise. In some cases, it's even possible that you land up talking to telesales personnel working to a script or a standard operating procedure - and they're quite possibly just reading the product blurb you also found on their site back to you.

"Design-your-own" sites

You might also find some "clever" websites - from anywhere - where you "design and decorate" your own product and add your own logo, click to buy, and then pay. These are very often for one-product companies, perhaps for t-shirts, or for lanyards - and they are deceptively and enticingly simple. However, you'll probably be surprised how time-consuming and difficult navigating these online design machines can be. Even if you do work out how to get the product to look more or less how you want it to, how can you be confident that the delivered product will look exactly like it did on the screen?

What could go wrong with your order?

Whilst you're thinking about who to buy from, it's worth thinking about some of the things that could go wrong, and trying to work out how you would handle these situations if you are dealing with an overseas factory direct or working with a purely web-based sales site.

The reality is that with any bespoke manufacturing process, there is enormous scope for something to go wrong. "Arm's length purchasing", especially the type when you do it all online with overseas factories, one-product firms, or multi-product stores - or with people you don't really know - is particularly prone to the types of problem which only come to light when your products have arrived, and there's no time to put it right. This can be very far indeed from the "click and buy - trouble-free" image they like to portray.

How are you going to sort out these problems?

Here's a list of some of the common headaches we've heard about when people have gone on their own to a direct factory contact or ordered from a remote web-based provider.

- Logo print poor - rubs off easily.
- Substandard or dangerous products - power adaptors which burn out or pens which leak in your pocket.
- Misspelling of simple text - the "Fighting Irish" misprinted as the "Figthing Irish" on a drink cup delivered to F+B outlets before a game.
- Logos printed incorrectly – elements missing or stretched bizarrely out of your "normal" proportions.
- Wrong print or product colours.
- Orders delivered after the date you need them for your event, in spite of constant emails and failed phone calls.
- Your friendly factory contacts keep your money and don't deliver your order – and because they are a long way away, it's just not practical or cost-effective for you to take action to do anything about it.

- Goods arrive - but the product itself is unacceptably and dramatically different from the sample or pre-production photo.
- Clear written instructions are interpreted exactly the opposite way to how you intended.
- Courier service personnel steal the goods in transit.
- The premium rate "Overnight" courier service you paid for actually takes four days or more, and the factory abdicates all responsibility saying they were only responsible for getting it into the courier service system – it's now down to you to try to track it down and sort out where the package is.
- The factory's preferred (i.e., cheapest) courier service misdirects your package to Shanghai instead of Hong Kong.
- Products just don't function – mugs leak, umbrellas don't close, or USB storage capacity is a fraction of its nominal rating.

All these things can happen even in well-established production operations – but the risk is even larger if you're producing a one-off product for a time-specific event.

If you're buying direct from a factory or hoping for the best with a website contact, it's going to be down to you to sort the mess out.

Finding A Promotional Product Specialist

My strongest recommendation is to find a Promotional Product Specialist who actually understands marketing, and at the same time can handle the sourcing of quality products. You need someone experienced in working with clients like you, who speaks your language, can help you work out which products are a good fit with your needs, and helps you manage the supply and sourcing in a pain-free and stress-free way. When people come to my company Synco Marketing via our home page or through referrals, this is the type of service we offer them.

You might buy cheaper if you buy direct, but when you work with a Promotional Product Expert your risk factor is comparatively very much lower – and you'll save time, money, and stress when something doesn't go 100% to plan. All the problems listed above are very real in any one-off manufacturing scenario, and Promotional Product Specialists have seen them all before. They have quality control (QC) systems, and inspections as part of their routine, and other operating procedures to minimize the likelihood of these problems occurring in the first place. And, unlike you, they live with these same or similar problems from day to day, and are used to finding ways to resolve them or minimise the impact for their clients if they do occur.

Googling "Promotional Products Marketing Expert" and the name of your home town will probably help you find a local advisor or two who you can contact without obligation.

Or better still, maybe you can get a personal recommendation? Talk to others in your industry or your contacts in other industries – who do they use? How about your local network groups, Chambers of Commerce etc – is there a specialist you can find there? Can you reach out to your LinkedIn contacts for advice?

Summary

In this chapter, we reviewed the decision you've taken to work with Promotional Products in a serious committed way, and helped you get clear on finding the right partner to help you with supply. Now work on the practical exercise to apply what you've learned, before moving on to Chapter 5 to review your pre-order preparations.

Practical Exercise

Take five minutes out from reading right now, go to the back of the book, or grab a piece of paper and think about :-

1) Who could be the Promotional Products Pro in your organisation. Should it be you? Or if not, who would you nominate to take this responsibility?

2) Who should you use to help you source your products? Do you have the resources and the time and energy to go it alone, or should you be contacting a Promotional Product Specialist to help you out?

Making sense so far?

Want to watch a quick video which helps to explain this some more?

As you know, this book is interactive, - to get free updates and bonus videos, access to more resources, and upgrades to the book when new versions or editions are released, visit www.getyournameoncoolstuff.com

or scan this QR code

and follow the instructions.

CHAPTER FIVE

Order Preparations - The Promo Pro's Approach To Getting Everything Right Before Placing The Order

A sports team needed a specific type of shirt for an event, and contacted their supplier about two or three months in advance.

Discussions went forward and back, and in the end, prices were confirmed and the order confirmed.

Unfortunately, the pre-order process didn't run smoothly – it proved impossible to get agreement on artwork in good time, because sponsors were being finalized all the way through the process, and each sponsor's expectations for their branding exposure had to be managed. This translated into delays getting hold of workable versions of sponsor logos, and then there were several revisions of the overall design, often with different combinations of new or different logos, and changes to their relative positioning on the garment.

Time was starting to run short.

Deciding on the number of shirts required in each size proved complex too. The factory provided charts that the client found hard to interpret, and in the end, pretty much at the last possible date that would still allow the factory the time they needed to produce the garments, the quantities needed in each size were finally confirmed.

Almost miraculously, the products were delivered on time, but in spite of this, everyone was disappointed.

The shirts were way too big.

The logos were way too small.

So what had gone wrong?

In the rush to get the garments into production, mistakes were made in understanding the sizing chart, and there was no time left before the critical event delivery date to produce and send sizing samples to ensure complete peace of mind.

Likewise with the logo sizing, there was already a lot of confusion just coming to an agreement on which logos to place where, and no-one thought to take the time to fix the actual size of each one. The logos looked to be a "reasonable" size on the original artwork supplied by the factory, but when this was turned into final production artwork, the logos were for some unknown reason reproduced much smaller – no-one at the factory or at the supplier spotted this change until everything was delivered.

Lessons from this experience?:-

1) *Make getting workable artwork a priority – the earlier the better.*
2) *Avoid requesting last minute changes unless they are "mission-critical" – these only add to the confusion and multiply the risk of further errors.*
3) *Make sure you agree on the dimensions of every logo in every position - and check them.*
4) *Make sure you budget for time to see pre-production samples or photos before final production is approved.*

5) *Be completely sure that everyone involved in the decision-making understands sizing charts – get sizing samples if you are at all unsure.*

This happened to one of our clients a good few years ago now, but they're not alone, and we hear stories like this from others in the industry very often. At our company, we're always on the lookout for learning points from situations like this so that we can further tighten up our own procedures and processes to make sure we really do help our clients get the best possible results.

We learned something really valuable from this experience – that as soon as real nagging time pressure starts to kick in, then the risk of misunderstandings, making mistakes, or forgetting things increases for everyone involved. Some suppliers take this so seriously that they simply refuse to take short delivery time business where there's a risk of this sort of situation arising.

Being properly prepared and working to a time frame which allows for reasonable rectifications and changes, whilst following a checklist which covers as many variables as you can foresee makes the whole experience more straightforward, and reduces the risk and stress for all involved.

Pre-order placement - the Promo Pro's approach to getting it right

In this chapter, I'm going to talk about what happens in the pre-order stage, and what you should think about when you are preparing to place your product order.

I'll work through the practical considerations, specific actions you need to take, and what to expect on the way. You'll learn insider secrets and tips that will save you time and energy - and maximise your chances of a successful campaign outcome with minimal stress in the process

Using checklists and procedures

You can achieve a lot more by having a clearly understood method. Whether you call it a system or a procedure or a way of working doesn't really matter, what's essential is that there is a way to do something that works well and ensures that nothing is forgotten. Having a procedure in place makes you naturally more methodical in your approach, and saves you time and effort by making sure you are getting more things right first time.

Checklists save you having to try to remember how you did it last time, and mean that there's no need to reinvent how to do it every time the same sort of job comes up. They help to keep you on track, make sure you have got all the elements you need to do the job, and reminds you about options when you need to decide on alternatives.

With a written procedure, you are clear about what to do, and in what order to do it every time, and this allows you to concentrate on the content and quality of your work. It saves time and energy, and means that when you come to the end of the task, you can have the pleasure of really crossing it off your list with the confidence that it has been done properly!

We're big fans of procedures and checklists in Synco, and we use them for scores of activities – daily ones as well as weekly and monthly ones. Even if your company doesn't insist on working this way, you'll see huge benefits if you personally adopt this approach by being able to do your own work more effectively and efficiently.

Use this checklist to make sure you cover all these areas when you're preparing to place your orders. Every time.

What and How - what do you want to achieve, and which product are you going to use?

I've talked about this in more detail before, but it's really important to review this once more when you are preparing a campaign so that you really are clear about where you're going. This means you need to :-

1) Clarify the basic objectives behind your campaign and your methodology – you did this in Chapters 1 and 2.
2) Have some clear idea about the type of product you are going to use, based on the above, your budget, timescale and target marketing attributes. We talked about this in Chapter 3.

Be ready with good quality workable logos and artwork

Artwork really matters. Poor artwork - e.g., logos, and other associated text like URLs and taglines in a format that your supplier cannot use, is no use.

For your logo, a small size jpg file is almost certainly going to be no good, so check now, and if that's all you have, then be advised that you'll almost certainly need something more. Usually promotional product suppliers will need Adobe Illustrator files with lines converted to Vectors – check NOW to see if you have these and if not, then take action to get hold of these file. Having easy access to these on file will make life much easier.

Unless you are a designer, it's unlikely that you will have Adobe Illustrator installed on your computer, and this can make it more difficult to read a Vector file. Often, it is possible though using Preview or by right-clicking on the file name but not every time. It's a good plan to ask your designer to also give you a PDF and a JPG of the same files (or a screenshot) so you can more easily view the content, and check that they are what you want. Send those screenshots and PDF and JPG files to your supplier too!

Call To Action and Contact details

Alongside your logo, you really should make it a part of your routine to review every time whether or not you need to include a Call to Action (CTA) and a Way to Get in Touch (WGT) on your product. This depends on your campaign, and how your item is to be used to support it. Typically thank-you gifts might have less overtly promotional content than items that are targeted at prospects or new leads.

For some smaller-sized items, it may or may not be practical to add a lot of text, so consider how to do this in other ways. Maybe you can use abbreviated texts or URLs, -or sometimes a QR code could work. If you like the idea of QR codes, you should know that some products are more difficult to print these on successfully - get some expert advice if you want to go down that route.

If you can't print enough information on the product itself to meet your campaign objectives, then can you print it on the packaging? Or can you add hangtags, a card, or a simple printed instruction sheet?

Keep it Simple (KISS)

Remember to be realistic about who you are and with whom you're connecting. If you are new to a market or a relatively small player, it's generally a good idea to make it very, very easy for people to easily see what you do and get in touch if they want. If you mystify or confuse them or make them search around for a way to contact you, you'll lose them quickly. Most of us don't have the patience to be intrigued and mystified! You've really got only a few seconds to make a connection, so if you make yourself too hard to understand, your prospect will very quickly move onto something else.

It's ok, of course, to use your company name if it's searchable, and that search pops us with your name at the top of the list. Otherwise it may be better to cut to the chase and just use a URL. You can certainly be a little creative about this. Can you create a short custom URL you could use to direct clients to your site if your normal URL has a longer name that's difficult to print on your product?

And check your generic home page - it might not be much help for what you're trying to do now – is that actually the best landing page to direct your clients to for this campaign? It costs very little to add an extra page to your existing site, so maybe you need a page to specifically support your campaign – or a lead page to collect emails before allowing further access?

Don't Disconnect!

I'd strongly recommend that you avoid using any text or images that might create a disconnect – smut or sleaze really is best avoided. Unless you're very sure of yourself and your brand, tend towards being more conservative in what you write on your product or on any accompanying literature, documents, hangtags, etc. Humour can be difficult to manage too, unless you are very confident about your copywriting skills and know that it will be well received – and not misinterpreted. It might seem a bit boring, but you really don't want to cause offence and give ammunition to potential critics. Steer clear of causing offense through any text or images you use.

Extra artwork elements

Apart from your logo, CTA, and Contact details you might be planning on adding other elements, like a tag line or a photo or some other graphical element on your product. If it's a photo, you'll need a high resolution file, probably higher than you would normally be comfortable emailing, so you might need to use a file sharing mechanism to handle this. Whatever the situation, it's best to have all this prepared and agreed internally early on in the process so that you can be ahead of the game.

You can probably get internal artwork help if you're in a big company - there might be someone who can help you out with the additional artwork elements you need for your Promotional Product Marketing Campaign. Inevitably, it may take longer than you expect to have a colleague help you out, so start "training" them early with requests for your normal company logo in AI format or other vector-artwork formats, so you can see how responsive and easy they are to work with.

Layout

It's important that you show the supplier how you expect the final product to look, so that they know how to position the logos and other design elements on the product.

Your supplier won't really be able to get going on this until they've got all your elements – so the earlier you can send your supplier all the artwork elements you are planning to use, the quicker they will be able to let you know if what you want is workable or not.

The easiest way to do this is to sketch it out with some explanatory notes, and send that to them along with the logo files and other design elements like photos, text, etc. If you are good with PowerPoint, or a similar programme, maybe you can use that to "draw" the approximate layout.

I'd recommend you specifically avoid using the words "logo here" to indicate where you want your logo to be printed. We've actually seen examples where communication has broken down to such an extent that those exact words "logo here" have been printed in the position requested (instead of the client logo) on the final product. Embarrassing all round!

Logo Sizing

Suppliers can't read your mind when you say you want a "big logo on the front" or "make it a bit smaller". You can save everyone a whole lot of time by simply stating what you want in real terms.

If you don't know what logo sizes you want, then the supplier will be able to make a suggestion. In this case again, I'd really recommend that you check any size they propose with a tape measure, to be sure that this will give you the design you want "in real life". If they suggest your shirt logo should be 4 cm wide, check it carefully. Is that actually going to be big enough to get your prospects' attention?

To be safe, you should assume that any artwork you receive will be NOT TO SCALE – more about this later too.

Go back to old-school, and check everything with a ruler - otherwise you might get a shock when the products are delivered.

Use cm or inches, but not a mixture of both! Be clear which you are using, and stay consistent, just using one system or the other for all measurements - mistakes can and do happen because of this!

Product Measurements and Scale

Don't fall into the trap of assuming that "standard" products are all the same size – they most definitely aren't!

Some years ago, a school ordered some scarves from us - we clearly mentioned the product size we planned to supply on all the correspondence. But when they were delivered, the client was surprised to find that they were actually quite a lot shorter than they expected – so much so that in fact they could hardly be tied round the neck.

We all checked on the paperwork, and the scarves were in fact supplied exactly as per the specs that had been offered by the factory and accepted in writing by the client. Unfortunately, no-one, ourselves included, had thought to actually get out a tape measure to see for themselves what that size really meant in practice and to visualize if that was "ok" or not.

It's more difficult than you think to estimate sizes accurately or to visualize measurements, without using some type of measuring device to check.

Make it your normal habit to use a ruler or a tape measure, and make a real effort to visualize any sizes referred to accurately. When your contact emails you a photo of a great looking coffee mug, and the text mentions that is 3" high, are you sure that's what you want? When dimensions are shown, it's always worth checking – do they sound right? And if they aren't given, you should ask for them, every time!

Packaging

Your supplier will need you to tell them how you want your products to be packaged – this can be an opportunity for additional branding, though this needs to be handled carefully.

Check how the products will be packaged, and if the proposed method doesn't work for you or your brand, then explore alternatives to find a solution. The "wrong" type of packaging might undermine the positive impact of an otherwise excellent gift.

Avoid anything that creates a disconnect between you and your product – for example if your company has a clear stance on environmental concerns, you'd want to avoid any packaging which could be considered "unnecessary".

Unless you're ordering a specific type of presentation packaging, it's very likely that the packaging supplied with your products is really only intended for basic protection after production and during delivery.

We're all trying to reduce the amount of poly bag waste, and because of this, you may prefer not to give your recipients a poly-bag wrapped product - but your supplier might not be as environmentally-aware as you are just yet, and they might use poly bag packaging as their normal solution for protecting products in transit. After all, that's what they have been doing for years without complaint. If you specify "no poly bag wrapping" from your supplier, you might risk receiving damaged goods if they don't yet have an alternative protection solution.

It is a good policy to request this from your suppliers if you feel strongly about it – and the more we all do this, the faster we will see alternative solutions in place – on the other hand, it also makes sense to be pragmatic and realistic. In practical terms, this means you might need to prepare yourself or your team to unpack or repack the products before you distribute them to your targets, if the packaging solution which you discover on delivery day turns out to be a mismatch.

You might also want to review the possible practical downsides if you decide to go without individual packaging – for example, if you're distributing thousands of t-shirts at an outdoor event and there's a thunderstorm, and the boxes are soaked through, would you rather be handling dry shirts in simple-to-manage sealed poly bags or constantly picking up and re-folding unwrapped shirts which are now all wet?

Adding more value with Packaging

For many products, you could seriously consider a more environmentally sound packaging solution than the typical "branded presentation box" or white paper box, which of course usually gets thrown away pretty soon in most cases. A microfibre drawstring pouch printed with a good design is a useful, re-useable eco-friendly alternative that may well work for you and your brand longer than the product contained within.

Digital Mockup for review

Sending the supplier your sketch instructions for the product layout is half the job. The other half is making sure that they send you their own factory artwork or "digital mockup" for you to approve. Make sure you get this for the packaging, as well as for your product.

This is your supplier's interpretation of your instructions, which they will use as their reference for production. Having the chance to review this mockup helps you be more confident they have understood exactly what you want – and should stop "logo here" being printed on your shirt! It's like asking someone to do something for you, then having them repeat back to you what you want them to do in their own words.

Be particularly careful about the impression you might get from a digital mockup, as these are **ALMOST NEVER** 100% to scale. Take note of any sizing indicated, and be sure to check with a ruler that you are happy with it.

You do really need to check this digital mockup carefully. If there are mistakes or misunderstandings, keep going back until you have it right - and keep a record of your formal approval. Make sure that any critical measurements are accurately recorded, and that PMS colour references are described correctly too. It's more important to get the written references to these correct, because the mockup is unlikely to be to scale, and colours will always show up differently on different computers and printers.

If you're in an organisation where the Head Office has to approve everything you do, then you might want to ask around, and see how long that usually takes. You don't want to be losing sleep over delivery because you had to delay placing the order thanks to the Head Office taking three weeks to approve your artwork. Be realistic up front, and don't expect much sympathy if you try to rush it through faster than usual - they will probably view this sort of request as low priority and do it in their own sweet time.

You've got a couple of options here if you have to go through the Head Office. You might decide not to tell them (as the old Cantonese saying goes - The Mountain is high and the Emperor is far away…). Or to be safe, plan this into your schedule, and allow more time than you think you need.

Quantity

Defining the right amount to buy is an art – there are no 100% correct answers.

If you buy a larger quantity, you can often get a lower unit price, and your one-off order costs are spread over a larger number of items, so it can work out as better value. However, if this ties up your funds and space unnecessarily, and you could have other uses for that money, then maybe the right decision would have been to buy less.

My usual recommendation is to avoid buying too much - if you must buy a lot more than your real need right now (calculate this based on the definite requirement you know about now, plus some extras for people who are going to inevitably want more) – try to keep the overbuy to a minimum, and aim to make the additional quantity more flexible.

Take this example:

You have 500 guests attending your product launch event, and the Minimum Order Quantity (MOQ) for your chosen product is 1,000 units.

First, you should double check if there is no further flexibility on the MOQ – sometimes your supplier can make an exception, so it's always worth double checking – you should be prepared to pay a higher unit price for a smaller quantity if they can accept it.

If that's really not possible, and you have to buy at least 1000 units, then try asking your supplier if you can order 530 (500 + an extra 30 units to give you a few spare) which are specifically branded with your company logo and the details for your URL and product launch. And have the other 470 branded more generically – perhaps with just with your logo and a phone number.

This way the extras are not tied to this product launch, and you can use them for other purposes in the future.

You may pay an extra setup cost for the split order of 1,000 units, but for the benefit of flexibility, it's probably well worthwhile.

Apparel Sizes

When you are buying apparel, this can be a headache. You will need to specify in detail how many products you need in which size.

Sizing can be confusing – partly because there's no real standard common approach, and because people in different parts of the world have different ideas about what is meant by "Small," "Medium," "Large," etc.

It's really your responsibility to make sure you read the supplier size charts correctly and interpret them correctly. But you should also expect your supplier to be able to help you out. If your supplier seems unhelpful or flippant about this, push them to give you better information and if they still don't help, you should take this as a danger signal.

If they aren't much help, you should probably shop around and see if another supplier will be more helpful. I was talking to a client the other day who had been putting up with substandard responses from suppliers on apparel sizing. The products are nice enough, but they had some problems with delivered sizes being different from what they expected. That's cost this company the business – my client's now looking to move on from that supplier to find someone who will actually help them solve these sizing questions together with them.

Checking Size Charts

Make sure your supplier sends you size charts, and read these carefully to make sure you really understand them. Check particularly to see if the measurements refer to the garment size or to the measurements of the person who will wear it. Very often the measurements shown on a size chart are those of the garment itself, though this is not necessarily true for every supplier. Note that this is different from what you may be used to when you buy off-the-peg clothing in the mall.

Also see if it's possible to get physical size sets of sample garments so a few people in your organisation can try them on, and help you determine how they fit.

If you can't get a sample size set, here's a practical way forward for standard items like tees and polos, to determine if your supplier's sizes are "bigger" or "smaller" than what you think of as "normal".

First, find a shirt from your own wardrobe that you like, and that fits you comfortably. Next, take a tape measure and check the actual size of your own shirt in the same way as is shown on the size chart. It is probably easiest to use the measurement across the chest. Then take this measurement, and check where this size appears on your supplier's size chart.

Whilst you might think of yourself as a "Medium", the product that actually fits you from your new supplier's size chart could be classified differently - maybe as a Small or maybe as a Large. Knowing where you fit on their size chart helps you get a feel for how they position themselves and whether the supplier sizes are larger or smaller than your expectations – if their sizes are larger than "normal" you might want to order smaller sizes, if smaller than "normal" then you should probably skew the order more towards larger sizes.

Quality Control – will you get what you ordered?

It's reasonable for you to expect that your order will be delivered in conformance with the specific details you agreed with the supplier.

Some simple examples:-

You ordered green bags – *are they the correct shade of green in conformance to the PANTONE reference number you ordered?*

You ordered 3mm thick mousemats – *are they all really 3mm thick?*

You ordered t-shirts for an event – *is the logo printed correctly, and are the shirts which are labelled "L" actually the right dimensions according to the "L" column on the size chart?*

Check with your supplier about how they arrange this type of pre-dispatch visual QC check so that you are comfortable that they are treating this issue seriously. Serious suppliers have their own "self-inspection" quality control, and if you wish, they (or you) can also employ third-party inspection companies to inspect products pre-dispatch at the production location on your behalf.

Do you need to plan for Product Testing?

There may be additional local legal requirements relating to the sale, distribution, or use of any Promotional Products you choose. These vary, depending on the type of use your products are intended for and where you intend to use them. Your supplier may not necessarily know what these requirements are in your specific situation, so it is best if you can find out what is needed by asking a local source you trust, and discuss this with your supplier to be sure you do both understand what's required.

Meeting these requirements often implies more complex tests than a visual QC inspection. It is possible to test for a huge range of performance attributes or specifications which are related to the manufacturing process, such as toxicity of any inks used, absence of known carcinogenic elements, and whether a plastic drinking vessel really is BPA-free. In fabrics, you might consider tests for trace elements in dyes, verification of the fabric weight and composition, performance issues such as dry-wicking or UV protection rating values. For electronic items, there are performance and safety tests you can apply.

What if it fails?

This type of order-specific product testing comes at a financial cost, and there is always a risk of a failure – which could then entail further costs in re-testing, as well as delivery delay if you decide you need to have any mistakes rectified or new products produced to replace those which have failed a test.

However, let's not lose sight of the fact that the whole purpose of testing is precisely to avoid future major headaches that may come from having your name and logo on out-of-spec or dangerous products. Bearing this in mind, you may decide that the risk of some delay in delivery in the case of a test failure is a small price to pay for that peace of mind. This is another good reason why it's so important to organise yourself in plenty of time and have some flexibility built into your schedule.

If you are more comfortable with having specific assurances like this, and want to be sure that Your Name is on genuinely Cool Stuff (that's properly tested and approved), then you should talk to your supplier to understand how they manage this, and work out how to best proceed in your situation.

Which Delivery Date do you mean?

You should be very clear about communicating any dates which relate to your order – depending on your position in the supply relationship and your point of view, "delivery date" can mean different things to different people.

At Synco Marketing here in Hong Kong, we are very conscious of this distinction - there might be up to five different dates which might be called "delivery dates" by different people involved in the order. It all depends on your point of view.

1. The date the supplier has promised to have production finished at their factory.
2. The date the supplier has committed to have the products delivered to our office.
3. The date the factory has committed to have the products delivered to our client (when the factory is handling the shipping direct to client on our behalf).

4. The date we have agreed with the client on or before which they will receive the goods.

5. The CCED (Client Critical Event Date) – if we know about one. This is the date of an event where the products will be used. Also known as the "drop-dead" date. When there is a CCED, we all understand that if the order is delivered after this date, then the products will be considered as effectively useless, and the campaign will have failed.

When do you need the order delivered?

It is good practice for all involved to negotiate a firm agreement on delivery dates.

If your instructions are to order some gifts to be delivered "as soon as possible", this isn't really very helpful for anyone. If "as soon as possible", in your mind means "sometime next month" – and the next possible delivery your supplier can commit to is in three months time, then you have an immediate disconnect. If you don't really know when the products are needed, try to get a more specific answer from your internal sources, and get this cleared up before it becomes an unwelcome surprise.

In case the answer does really turn out to be "whenever you can, it's not urgent", then it's still worth trying to probe further to see if there are events coming up in one-to-three months time. You'd be surprised at how often we get calls from clients who initially said "just deliver when you can", and then call again a week or so into the production process to say "please just make sure you get them to us by Tuesday next week because we've just realized we've got an Event and we'd like to use them then".

If you can predict that there will be opportunities where products might be useful and there's a chance that someone is going to ask for them – then it could well be worth trying to fix that date as the target with your supplier.

Always agree on a target date

There might be times when you really don't have a critical event date, and you're genuinely happy to let your supplier deliver to you on the basis of "whenever you can is OK, we're not in a rush".

In cases like these, to actually make your life easier, and for better supplier control and monitoring, I suggest that you make a clear agreement about a specific date deadline with your supplier anyway. This way, you can monitor how good they are at meeting delivery promises and keeping their word.

Your supplier really won't mind working to a deadline if it's within their capability, and in fact, good suppliers will welcome this as their chance to prove to you how efficient they can be at doing what you ask – if they seem less enthusiastic, then that may give you a clue about their commitment to customer service and delivery accuracy.

There's no need to push a supplier to a date they are not comfortable with, so agree on a target delivery date that suits them. It might feel like you are setting a deadline when it's not necessary, but doing this is very useful – a good supplier should be capable of keeping to a timeframe which they have agreed to, so why not test them out? Your next order might be really time critical, and you'd want to be confident that your supplier is capable of meeting what they say they can do.

If the supplier does runs into a problem on delivery when you've set them a deadline of your own making, then there's no need to be difficult about it. You can be accommodating and forgiving, and cut them some slack this time. Good suppliers will love you for this approach, and be more willing to go the extra mile for you next time around when delivery dates might be more critical.

Critical Event Dates

If you do have a real target date for when you need your products, you'll need to work out how long you will need to check and prepare the products for use prior to that date, then add in some buffer to take account of the risk of possible transit delays, and then define that as your delivery date. Don't be casual about this, it is really important to be very precise.

Precision is everything here - you aren't doing yourself any favours if all you do is tell your supplier "we need it for our event on the 16th". If you just mention one date, human nature means that your supplier is likely to just focus on the date mentioned. There is a pretty good chance that your supplier will even enter this in their order book as "deliver on 16th".

When someone at the supplier's office looks at that same note a few weeks later, they might well understand from it that it's ok to plan to deliver sometime before 6.30 p.m. on the 16th. But if your event is planned for 9 a.m, on the 16th, that will be too late. In this case it would have been better to have given the supplier some more precise detail.

It sounds obvious, but this kind of miscommunication happens very easily and very often, so do yourself a favour, and do a bit of extra thinking for your supplier.

You know better than they do what you need to do with the products before you can use them – and if you can tell your supplier the different key dates that are involved in your campaign preparation, and what that means for delivery, then that will help them understand the full picture. As a bonus, you will have a much better chance of getting the products delivered when you want them.

Be date-specific, not day-specific

Don't forget to be sure that you are all talking the same language – specific dates work best. The "number of days it takes to produce" or "days elapsed" is a useful guide when you are negotiating an order, but it's best to tie it down to a specific date and have any misunderstandings cleared up early when you're signing orders. Otherwise, there's a big risk you will discover a miscommunication when it's too late to do anything about it, and your delivery is going to miss the event it was intended for.

Misunderstandings can arise through "working days" or "calendar days". Here's an example we see often – on the order documentation or quote it might say something like "Delivery 10 days" – but does that mean 10 working days or 10 calendar days? Is that including or excluding public holidays? Starting from when?

It's really best to use a phrase stating the actual place and dates - "delivery to buyer's office address on or before 10th November" - so everyone is very clear.

Logistics and Delivery

What's going to actually happen when the products are delivered?

How much space have you got to use, and is it OK for you to store products there? Can you visualise how much space you will need for that order of A4 sized portfolios?

Can you put them all in your office, or do you need to use someone else's space?

Think about your space availability, and plan accordingly either to get the right amount of storage room or to adjust your planned order quantity.

You may also need to work out how to get the products to the final destination if it's an offsite event – can it go in someone's car or a taxi? Or will you need to get a man in a van?

If you are getting products that are to be used on a "Critical Event Date", you can't afford to cut it too fine, because if they arrive too late, then it really is too late. On the other hand, you probably don't want the products delivered too early if this means you'll be falling all over them in the office for weeks on end. Try to visualize what you'll be receiving and when, and plan accordingly. You might be willing to put up with a few boxes for a day or so, but not a container load of gear for weeks on end.

Scheduling delivery or storage

Take action now and decide where you will need to put delivered products and how long for. This might need some internal negotiation and discussion so make this happen. Don't leave it till the boxes arrive and try to sort it out then, it is better to manage expectations internally if you're going to need some help from your colleagues in a few weeks time when your products arrive.

Talk with your supplier about this – they may be willing to hold on to the goods for you, or possibly you can have them deliver direct to your venue and have the venue store for you. This can be risky, and you need to make sure that the venue is genuinely ok to do this for you - we've delivered product to venues for clients in the past when requirements haven't been properly confirmed, and the venue has refused to sign for the delivery.

If it looks as though products may arrive earlier than needed, and that's going to cause you a storage problem, maybe you can ask your supplier to first confirm with you before they ship. That would be better than just letting them ship whenever they feel like it. You might think it's a good idea to try some old tricks like deliberately withholding final payment to stop them delivering early (or by holding back on confirming the final delivery address details), but it's really better to have the discussion with them about exactly what you'd like them to do – your suppliers have had these tricks played on them before, and they don't appreciate it.

You could also try a Just-In-Time tactic whereby you hold back your order placement so that you time it "just right" – but that's extremely risky. This sort of approach might work in small batch orders in mass production environments where there are daily purchases and even hourly deliveries and a constant flow of product. With most Promotional Product requirements, it's a one-off purchase, and there will be too many variables to allow you to be 100% confident about the exact delivery date outcome. Remember that it only takes one unexpected problem to throw the delivery time. If you deliberately held back on placing the order just to avoid storing a few boxes in your office for a couple of weeks, and the order ends up arriving after your Critical Event Date because of this, then you're going to look foolish.

Estimate, Terms and Conditions, and Order Placement

When you're good to go with the above and have an Offer (or a more formal Estimate or Quote) from a supplier you are happy with, you should be ok to place the Order.

If you need advice prior to signing a contract that commits you to the supplier's Terms and Conditions of Sale, remember that this will almost certainly take more time. You should allow for that too.

Your supplier is unlikely to accept your order or start production until you have signed an order - and if you suddenly discover areas where you need to negotiate, this will delay things. You won't be happy if this delays your order confirmation so much that the original targeted delivery date cannot be met. If you can predict this being an issue, be proactive earlier in the process. Ask your supplier to send you their Terms and Conditions so you can have your advisers review these early. That way, they can ask the necessary questions and agree on any amendments needed from your side before this impacts on delivery time.

Otherwise, make sure all product, pricing, and delivery details are correct on your offer, and get it signed off and confirmed back to the supplier. Many will need some payment in advance before they can commence production, so be prepared to make this happen.

In Summary

In this chapter, we've looked at the steps to go through, and the options to consider when preparing your order. We've worked through all the elements to review as a checklist to help you make this process more systematic, and covered how to include a call to action and ways to get in touch, overall design and layout, text, logos, digital mockups, packaging options, product measurements, garment and decoration sizing, delivery dates, logistics, scheduling, and confirming the order.

Practical Exercise

Now, once again take five minutes out from reading right now, go to the back of the book, grab a piece of paper, and work through all the elements you're going to need to have in place for the product you choose for your campaign.

Do you have what you need in place?

Do you know how you can get it?

Take action now to review this, and for the items you can't find or don't know set yourself an action task in your calendar sometime in the next week to be sure you make it happen :-

Pre-order Checklist

- What and How - what do you want to achieve, and which product are you going to use?
- Be ready with good quality workable logos and artwork.
- Call To Action and Contact details (Keep it Simple).
- Don't Disconnect!
- Extra artwork elements.
- Layout.
- Logo Sizing.
- Product Measurements and Scale.
- Packaging – and adding more value with Packaging.
- Digital Mockup for review.
- Quantity.
- Apparel Sizes.
- Checking Size Charts.
- Quality Control – will you get what you ordered?
- Do you need to plan for Product Testing?
- What is the backup plan if it fails?
- Which Delivery Date do you mean - agree a target date.
- Critical Event Dates - date-specific, not day-specific.
- Logistics and Delivery arrangements.
- Scheduling delivery or storage.
- Estimate, Terms and Conditions, and Order Placement.

Let's get Busy!

Download soft copies so you can easily print out the checklist, and get free updates and bonus videos, access to more resources, and upgrades to the book when new versions or editions are released.

Visit www.getyournameoncoolstuff.com

or scan this QR code

and follow the instructions.

CHAPTER SIX

Order Progress And Delivery

Here's a story about someone who needed promo items for their company to give to visitors at an upcoming event, and very nearly didn't make the delivery happen, even though the order should have been good to go. This is how Adam risked it all for the sake of a poly bag.

"Adam" knew he had to Get His Name on Cool Stuff for a specific event. He kicked things off well by talking to a supplier plenty of time before the event date, and requested lots of different alternative options. He reviewed plenty of samples, and liked some, didn't like others, and so on. He took a bit of time over this and finally, now with not so much time left, he decided on a product he liked, and started to haggle over the price. It was a low budget item, and he needed a relatively small quantity, but in this case it took longer than usual for him to agree a price. He also wasn't really sure how many units he actually wanted to buy, so this confused the supplier, and delayed the process some more.

The deadline for the event was getting closer and closer, but he still wouldn't formally confirm his order yet. This was because Adam wanted to talk about packaging.

Now of course, it's right to discuss all aspects of an order in advance, and the quality of the product is important. It does need to be functional, and the essential elements of the design had to be properly in place, to allow the Product to effectively get its message across to recipients, thereby maximizing the chances of the campaign's success.

But with hardly any time left to formally confirm the order in time to meet the delivery deadline for the event, Adam took the surprising decision to start up a debate the type of poly bag packaging the supplier was going to use.

Now, a poly bag is the usual standard of packaging for this level of budget item – it's simply intended to be used for delivery protection and ease of handling. A bag like this is usually discarded prior to, or immediately on, presentation. Nevertheless Adam felt that this was a key feature of the product that had to be "right", so pictures and samples were sent. After more days of indecision, the factory standard poly bag was rejected as unsuitable, and Adam selected a more costly alternative.

Time out! Reality check required here!

How "mission critical" was it to have the perfect "nice" poly bag for that product?

In terms of campaign objectives, what could actually have gone wrong if the gift (note this is a gift, not a retail item) had been packaged in the "wrong" type of poly bag?

Could this really have had any impact at all on the outcome of Adam's campaign?

Specifically, would Adam's contacts think any less of his company because of this poly bag?

Would they convert fewer leads because the poly bag offended people somehow?

Would Adam be unable to distribute some of his gifts to his prospects because of the bag?

Would people actually reject Adam's gift because of the bag?

Would his clients reduce their spending with the firm because of the bag?

Would this poly bag mean Adam became a joke amongst his peers working for other companies at the same event?

All unlikely!

But what if Adam failed to get any products at all for that event because he was tying himself up in knots over irrelevant elements of the product design (and because of this, he delayed confirming the order till it was too late to get the products delivered in time)?

YES, that would very significantly impact!

So this message goes out to you, Adam and your friends out there reading this book, be realistic and pragmatic when you are Getting Your Name on Cool Stuff. Focus on what you are trying to achieve, keep your specific overriding campaign objectives in mind, and don't let irrelevancies distract you from making sure that you have a workable product available when you need it.

Order progress – making the delivery happen

In this chapter we're going to run through the practical steps of what happens once you set your order in motion and confirmed it with the supplier. We'll run through what you need to keep track of, the milestones in the process where you'll need to be ready to review and approve submissions from the supplier and how to approach and resolve the situation if there's an unexpected and unwelcome delay, or some other problem.

Order placed – "in production" checks

Once the order is placed, there are a few things to keep track of. At this point, the ball passes to the supplier for them to prepare and execute the next phases of the process. For you, this should be the easy part, and this respite will allow you to focus and concentrate on the other parts of your campaign which need attention. If it is an event, you'll be handling the venue, catering, entertainment, the guest invitations, and so on, or for other types of campaigns you need to prepare support materials such as Call to Action automatic responses or dedicated websites.

Digital Mockup Approval

You might think that the "order clock" starts ticking as soon as you confirm your order, but many suppliers are unwilling to start any work on your project until they have a clear agreement on workable artwork, a signed commitment, and a cleared payment. If you are slow confirming or acting on these elements, this will have a knock-on effect on your delivery date.

It's easy to see why nothing can really start until the digital mockup is confirmed. You may have approved a mock-up already, or at least started the process in the pre-order stage, but if not, then now is the time to complete it as quickly as you can. In fairness, the factory can't start preparing to manufacture for you until they really know what they are supposed to be making. To minimize any possible disconnect, or unexpected "delay", it's good to be prompt when the supplier asks you to approve their mockup.

It can be a major cause of frustration if clients don't understand this. We've seen situations where a client confirms an order believing that they will receive products in three weeks, but then it takes them a further two weeks to supply the artwork.

When they're told it will now take a further three weeks from that date that the artwork was received, they get upset.

For a Promotional Product Pro like you, this shouldn't be the case! Make sure that you have your artwork and sketch prepared properly in the pre-order phase as we talked about in the previous chapter, and set yourself up so that you can review initial factory mockups quickly. Be aware and plan accordingly!

Pre-Production Sample (PPS) - follow up

Once you have approved the digital mockup, you might have the option of going straight to full production. In fact, if you are very limited in time for whatever reason, you may have to do this. Be aware, though, that this carries significant risks.

A much safer strategy is to review an initial sample produced by the factory, to be sure that your instructions have been correctly interpreted, and that the product is indeed the one you are expecting to receive. At Synco Marketing, we do usually recommend a review of a Pre Production Sample (PPS) before approving full production. We routinely arrange for our partner factories to provide a PPS, prior to full production approval so that everyone is clear about what is intended and how the final product is expected to look.

Normally, you should have an indication from your supplier on how long it should take to get you the PPS. Set yourself a simple reminder in your calendar when you'd expect to be seeing this, so you can check in with your supplier to be sure everything is on track. If it seems to be taking longer than you expect, this might be a cause for concern, so it's worth checking in to monitor this proactively.

Reviews can be actioned using photographs taken by the factory showing the Pre-Production sample and offering evidence that sizes and colours are correct. Pictures should show a ruler, and allow you to compare colours against the relevant pages of a PANTONE colour book. You may prefer to also get hold of this physical sample so you can see it for yourself to be sure it really is what you were expecting before giving your approval – or this can be something you trust your Promotional Products Specialist to handle for you on your behalf.

For apparel orders, this might be a simple strike-off of the screen print or sublimation print or embroidery on a fabric swatch sample, rather than a full final assembled garment. Again, insist on seeing measurements and colour comparisons so you can check against the agreed specifications.

PPS review

Review the sample against the agreed digital mockup and any other information you have conveyed to the supplier about how the product should look. Check this very carefully.

If you can spot inconsistencies or errors, raise them straight away, and discuss with your supplier about how they will resolve these in the final production run. It's at this point where - in spite of an apparently on-spec digital mockup - you might be spotting rogue mistakes or text and logos printed in the wrong colours, the wrong dimensions, or the wrong places. It is NOT SAFE to assume that because the digital mockup was approved and looked ok, then the PPS will be ok too. Mistakes and errors can slip in between these two milestones, so be diligent with your checking.

If you need to be sure that the corrections you have requested are made before full production, you might want to request a second PPS before final production approval. Of course, you need to be aware that this will take more time, and may impact on the final delivery date for production.

A more risky strategy, which is sometimes inevitable in the face of a tight deadline, is to give approval for production "subject to correction of defects" and clearly list the corrections required. Clearly, you run less of a risk in situations where the corrections or improvements you request are minor, or not mission-critical.

PPS – your last chance to make a change

This milestone represents your last chance to confirm and check that this product really is exactly what you want, before you set your supplier running to make the full production volume. So, if it turns out now that this is NOT what you really want, and you really do need to make a change and request a variation from what was previously approved, you should act now.

Don't take this step lightly though, and make sure you consider the implications. If you can live with the PPS as it is without further changes, you will simplify the process for yourself, and minimize the risks of further complications. You also need to be sure you really have the time and flexibility to manage this change, and cope with a possible delayed delivery. Remember, there will also be some financial penalty for doing this, because of additional set up charges the factory will incur to take account of any changes.

Having said this, there could be very valid, "mission-critical" reasons which do require you to make a change at this point. It could be that maybe someone in the firm has let you know about a new URL they need to have featured as part of the Call to Action for the upcoming event. In this case, you do have a chance to change this before thousands are printed "wrong".

Or if a new co-sponsor comes on board at the last minute, and you have to add their logo too – you could do that at this stage.

Or maybe the service showcased on this Promotional Product has in the meantime enjoyed some overnight success, and you want to build on this by adding something to the artwork design (incorporating "as seen on TV" / "# 1 bestseller"). Well, now is the time to check if it's possible.

If, for some reason, you have a change of heart about the product itself this is also your final opportunity to make this change.

So, whilst we really don't recommend changing product specs at this point in the process, it is technically feasible to do so. If you really do need to do it, then have an open discussion with your supplier to work out the right solution. Accept that there are likely to be additional costs and some increase to the delivery time, and consider these as the price you pay for additional flexibility. If you do need to make a dramatic change, at least you have this option. Work together with your supplier and whoever is running your campaign, to manage expectations and find compromises where you can.

Order Tracking

Different suppliers have different ways of letting you know how things are going with your order – we call this Order Tracking. Some are great at it, and constantly keep you up to date, whilst others are absolutely appalling.

I like to classify the suppliers we work with into three types –

- DIY Tracking
- Quality Information
- The Silent Treatment

You can guess from how each one typically behaves - which one would you prefer to work with?

Be active in the process

Whichever type of Tracking is your supplier's natural style, your best policy is to take a line of positive communication and interaction with them.

It doesn't have to take up a lot of time and effort on your part. You just need to show that you care about what they are doing for you. It's certainly worth keeping in contact with your supplier as your order progresses, even if it's just to show them that you are serious about the outcome, and that you respect the hard work they are putting in to help you get the fantastic products you have planned together. A good supplier will respond positively to this, and welcome customers who care enough to keep a track on their orders.

Suppliers like this relish the chance to prove to you again and again how good they can be. They know that if you care about the orders you place, and are delighted with what you get, then you are more likely to buy again, and also to recommend and refer them to your peers. It's true - they really do want to work more with you, and with more clients like you.

Keeping in touch with your supplier should not be confused with "aggressive expediting". This term is used in procurement circles to describe the practice of buyers communicating with suppliers specifically to try to speed up delivery of ordered products.

Some buyers find it tempting to go too far with this, and some even fall into the trap of shameless bullying. Exploiting what they perceive to be their superior position in the buyer-supplier relationship, they push suppliers to over-commit to unworkable delivery requirements. On occasion, they even resort to this to cover up their own or their organisation's incompetence in placing orders too late, or in wrongly predicting their needs.

Requests for help to get a client out of a tight spot are welcome, of course, but I've an instinctive aversion to this sort of buyer behaviour - as do all reasonable and serious suppliers.

Feel free to follow up positively on your order, but be careful not to get a name for yourself as an aggressive and habitual expeditor!

In Production – what can you do now?

Actually, there's not much more to do once you've approved that all is good to go for final production - at this point in time, it's all about your supplier making things happen for you. You can use this time to make sure that everything is fixed in your business so that you are ready to handle the products when they are delivered, and to make any final preparations with your distribution plan – that way, it won't all be a surprise and a panic when your order arrives.

Check on payment

Use this time to keep up to speed with what's happening on any payments due to your supplier, especially if someone else in your organisation is handling this. It's good to be sure that you have paid your supplier in accordance with their invoicing terms. If their terms require an initial payment before production starts, or a final payment prior to dispatch - and you've agreed that when you gave the go-ahead on your order - then it's fair to make sure that happens. Your supplier would be perfectly within their right to withhold shipment until payment is received in a case like this – and many will do this, so manage this situation proactively rather than letting it turn into a crisis at the last minute.

It's good form, and sound business etiquette, to ensure that you look after the payment to your supplier as carefully as you would expect them to look after your order. Clients who hide behind a slow-moving corporate accounts department, or deliberately delay payments themselves with excuses or silence get noticed - especially in business environments where most people do play by the rules. You don't want to get a name as a poor payer with your business partners so, even if it's your accounts department who are slowing things down, it's down to you – not your supplier - to ease things along internally and help push the payments through.

Production Delays

With so many elements to control in this type of production process, there's always a risk that something will go wrong during the production process which may incur some unexpected setback and a possible knock-on delivery delay. Being up front with your schedule is crucial to building a good relationship with your supplier - this way, you're more likely to have them working with you to solve your common problem if there's some slippage.

When this happens, it is always better to be in a good relationship with your supplier. Going straight to the finger-pointing blame game, and searching back through email history to "prove" who is at fault is not always productive! Of course, it's important to understand how a miscommunication happened when you look back, but when there's a problem right now, you want the focus to be on fixing it in a positive and cooperative way so that you can aim to minimize the fallout. Fix the problems first, and then tweak procedures collaboratively to help avoid them another time.

If you're dealing with larger volumes of product and shipping longer distances, the whole business of delivery scheduling gets even more exciting, more complex - and as the delivery date draws closer – more tense. A day's dispatch delay with a local delivery usually translates into just one day's delay on arrival. But if you're talking about larger volumes, and you're shipping by container from one continent to another, where the delivery journey time itself takes weeks rather than hours, the implications can be more serious. For example, there may only be one ship leaving for your destination port every week. In a case like this, if your supplier's factory misses the target shipping date by just one day, then your order could be stuck at the port for a week waiting for the next sailing – which means the impact of that on arrival date is multiplied by up to at least a week.

Ways to deal with delays include:

- Can the factory ship an initial proportion of the delivery by a faster method?
- Can you accept an alternative product, or an amendment to the design, which would then mean production can be completed on time?
- Is it feasible to push back your campaign / event to suit the new expected delivery date?
- Is there another supplier who can offer you a small quantity of an alternative product to keep you going in the interim?

When they occur, deal with delays professionally and keep your cool!

Inspection and Testing

When production is almost complete, any visual and QC tests you have agreed on will need to take place. If the supplier is handling this for you, you may hear from them if there is a problem. You usually get to hear this in the form of a message announcing a possible delay in dispatch because they spotted a problem which they want to fix.

If you're getting the results yourself from your independent testing house, you will need to review. Assuming everything has passed, it's of course a simple decision to allow production and dispatch to continue.

If your order has failed inspection or testing, you will need to review how serious the failure is, discuss with the supplier what the next steps would be to resolve the situation, assess and quantify the implications in terms of cost and time for each, and agree on a way forward.

Delivery

You'll be on top of this, of course, by now, as you will have been in contact with your supplier, and following up on the progress of your order in production.

If your supplier is also arranging delivery to your location, they should proactively keep you up to date with shipping and delivery details, so that you will have a good idea of the date and time the order will arrive.

Not all suppliers arrange the shipping for you from the factory, although most can and do sell on this basis. In some cases, it may make more sense for you to handle this yourself if you have a particularly good relationship with your local shipping / courier service.

The order's arrived! Check it now!

When the order is delivered, it really is best to check carefully that everything is there as ordered, and have a random check to be sure that everything looks right. You'll have probably been asked to sign a delivery note (or your representative will have done so if you weren't there to receive the products yourself). Your signature on this is usually taken as your confirmation that the delivery has been received in good condition. In practical terms, it is very difficult to confirm this when the courier is waiting for you to sign the paperwork, so it makes sense to quickly revert on this direct to the supplier if you find there's a problem.

Some suppliers will try to limit their exposure to complaints, if you don't let them know straight away if there's a problem. From a legal perspective, I'm not sure how well that stands up, but in those rare cases where there is a genuine problem, in practical terms, it really is in your interests to know about it from the get-go, so you can start working on a solution now whilst there might still be time to fix it.

Seriously, you really do need to check carefully

You should be pretty confident that everything is fine, bearing in mind all the pre-order checks you made and the approvals, confirmations, and inspections that have gone before. However, you should still be wary of assuming that everything is fine.

It's no good finding out when you start handing out your t-shirts at the event that someone at your end has made a mistake with the sizes ordered, and that most of the shirts are only fit for giants. It's also dangerous to assume that your products will be exactly as you ordered, just because you've ordered them before and they were fine. You can't really be sure - what if the delivery agent dropped the boxes, or they got wet in transit and that's affected your products? Or if they put the wrong delivery sticker on the box, and you've ended up with someone else's order?

It really is better to check on arrival, or as soon as you practically can. Document any problems carefully with photos as you take items out of the box and email these across to your supplier straight away, rather than coming back to them a week or so later. If you leave it a few days, it's more difficult to be confident about where or how the problem happened. It's just good practice to take responsibility yourself here, and be assured that all is well.

A problem discovered on delivery really is a rare occurrence, especially if you've worked through all the previous steps we've talked about to get you this far. Nevertheless, for that time when it's not quite right, you do want to be ready to handle it like a true Promo Pro.

Be flexible with problems – don't sweat the small stuff

A large part of this book covers some of the things that might go wrong – and how you can plan for this and mitigate against these risks to a great extent by using a friendly supplier in whom you can trust, and who will look after your orders for you. All the checks and balances I recommend you to take will also help to reduce the risk of a disappointment when the products arrive.

However, as I also mentioned, inevitably at some stage or other, either in production or once the order has arrived, there may be a minor problem or discrepancy which puts you in a position of having to decide how to proceed.

Of course, you have a right to expect things to be done right the first time, but you should be pragmatic about this too – not everything does go right all the time.

When this happens, it may be worth taking a step back before you despair, lose your temper, or send everything back to the supplier in a rage. Think carefully about how significant the problem really is, and assess whether it will actually put the success of your campaign at risk.

Will this problem really affect my campaign outcome?

It really may not be worth the stress. Take a deep breath and consider the likely impact on your campaign - will its effectiveness be jeopardized by spending more time, effort, and money to solve this "problem"?

If the items are faulty, broken, or substandard, then it's right to simply reject them and arrange for a replacement as soon as possible. However, if the problem you find is not dangerous, or material, then it really is worth considering carefully how much fuss to make about it.

Remember also the Terms and Conditions of Sale you signed off on when you placed the order (did you read that document?). They almost certainly included a proviso to say that minor deviations in colour and specification are always possible, and that the supplier cannot be held responsible for these. If the problem is minor, in reality this means we'd be talking about a goodwill discussion and a negotiation, the outcome of which will depend on your relationship with the supplier.

Whilst it is ok to be a demanding buyer and to have high expectations, sometimes it's better not to overdo it – it is easy to become ridiculous. Consider your tolerance gap, and work with your supplier to find a solution that keeps your credibility and reputation intact and your relationship sweet (for next time, when maybe you're going to really need their help).

It's fine to assess your product based on aesthetics, but perhaps this doesn't need to be your overriding consideration every time. Misspellings would be unacceptable, and you should reject products with this problem; the same applies to non-functioning URL links or QR codes. On the other hand, what about more minor issues such as imprint colour variations, photos cropped slightly differently from how you expected, small changes in product specifications or colours, or minor font differences from the ones you approved?

Is it really "Mission Critical", for example, if your logo ends up printed in a slightly different shade from your target corporate Pantone reference colour? Will it mean that fewer people respond to your Call to Action? In reality, hardly anyone outside your company will notice or care, and if your Call to Action is effective, neither should anyone inside your company!

If you think that your recipients would be baffled, confused, insulted, nonplussed, or otherwise irritated by receiving your "not-to-spec" gift, then you should reject it. On the other hand, if in reality it would be perfectly acceptable, and just as effective in meeting its objectives, maybe the right thing to do is to swallow your pride, and just get on with the campaign.

Be pragmatic, and remember your campaign objectives

Keep things in perspective, and remember that in most cases your Promotional Product is not supposed to be an item of perfection and beauty in itself, but to be a tool to help you reach a business objective.

Think about the opportunity cost to you of delaying your campaign because the colour is "wrong" on the Call to Action text on your new pens? If doing this pushes back the day you can start to use your products, then you're missing out on the potential leads and sales that these products could have generated for you starting from that time. Is it really worth missing out on that for the sake of a colour change?

Don't let a minor discrepancy automatically stop you using the products or inhibit your actions. If you find a minor problem with your order, and you decide to go ahead anyway and not reject it, you can still point this out to the supplier, and ask them to put this right for you when you place your next order. If you ask them nicely, they might even offer you a discount for that re-order.

Give useful feedback, and be generous with referrals

When you're a Promotional Product Pro, part of your job is to build a positive relationship with the people who supply you. In the same way that you can decide which suppliers you work with, your suppliers also have a choice about whether or not they like the idea of working with you. There are plenty of variables in this, but on a personal level, most suppliers prefer to deal with personable clients, who give useful feedback and are generous with their referrals. So when you're buying, be mindful of this, and think about how you can actually promote yourself and your company in such a way as to add value for your suppliers in a way that they will appreciate.

In Summary

In this chapter, we've looked at the steps to go through, and the options to consider whilst your order is confirmed and in the hands of the supplier. We've again worked through all the elements to review, and set them out as a checklist to help you make this process more systematic.

Practical Exercise

Now, once again, take five minutes out from reading right now, go to the back of the book, grab a piece of paper, and look through the reminder here of the contents from this chapter.

Take action now to review each point – there's probably not much you can prepare for until you're actually working on an order of your own, but jot down any keywords to prompt you to keep these in mind for the future.

- Digital Mockup Approval.
- Pre-Production Sample (PPS) - follow up and review.
- PPS – your last chance to make a change,
- Order Tracking - be active in the process.
- In Production – what can you do now?
- Check on payment.

- Production Delays.
- Inspection and Testing.
- Delivery.
- The order's arrived! Check it now!
- Be flexible with problems – don't sweat the small stuff.
- Be pragmatic, and remember your campaign objectives.
- Give useful feedback, and be generous with referrals.

By now, if you've followed all the steps in the book, you should be sitting with a good stack of quality products ready for action - and be all set to start your campaign.

Well done for getting this far!

If you haven't registered yet for the extra bonus materials and white papers connected with Get Your Name on Cool Stuff, then do it now.

Visit www.getyournameoncoolstuff.com

or scan this QR code

and follow the instructions.

CHAPTER SEVEN

Measuring Success

I asked a client the other day about their rationale for using promotional items.

"It's really just about getting the brand out there", they said.

So I asked how effective that was.

There was a bit of an embarrassed laugh, and then "Don't know, we can't really measure it".

So then we got to talking about ways they could perhaps measure it – and in fact, it turned out they had, almost by accident, gone some of the way to do this already.

The good news is that they had added a QR code onto their promotional product. Unfortunately, it turned out that this code just directed clients to their usual homepage.

Result?

- *No way to isolate the results and measure the impact of that particular campaign.*
- *No way to capture information about the recipients of their Promotional item (these were recipients who were already engaged enough and interested enough to try out the QR).*

- *No way to specifically capitalise on that goodwill and respond personally to the interest of some very engaged prospects – or to offer them something extra to keep them engaged further.*

When you're spending time and effort on marketing campaigns using Promotional Products, it really does make sense to try to get a handle on how effective it all is. Wouldn't you want to know if your campaigns are working? Or compare different approaches to see which gives the best results?

Measuring Success

I've often had clients ask me to explain how to work a cost-benefit analysis so they can decide whether Promotional Product Marketing is actually going to help them be more profitable. In this chapter, I'm going to talk about why measuring marketing of all types is challenging, but why it's still worth making an attempt to do it. I'll also be reviewing some simple ways that you can start to measure and analyse your own Promotional Product Marketing results.

Why Measuring Marketing Results is Difficult

Measuring the economic value of marketing activity is difficult because to put it simply, it's just not an exact science. It's hard to calculate a hard dollar-value return on investment with confidence, irrespective of the form of advertising, whether billboards, print ads, TV and radio, social media, or promotional products.

A traditional approach

There is much academic research on how to do this better, however, the traditional ways to measure the effective of advertising tends to work on the following premise.

- **Advertising** builds **Awareness.**
- In time, **Awareness** leads to **Sales.**

Therefore… **Advertising** builds **Sales**

Whilst this is appealing in its simplicity, measuring this correlation is more complicated. It's hard enough to measure past historical performance – but it's another huge increase in complexity to accurately predict the increased advertising spending needed to generate a specific desired increase in sales.

One of the difficulties lies in the measurement itself – whilst "sales" should be a straightforward quantifiable hard number, it's much harder to put a value on "awareness". Even the best measurements of "awareness" often rely on people's subjective responses to questionnaires or polls of sample populations. Getting this data may be costly and time-consuming. There may also be bias in the results, depending on who is asked to take part in the surveys, and who is willing to respond. "Awareness" is also influenced by external and environmental factors, for example, other mainstream advertising campaigns, or particularly aggressive - or unusually passive - competitor activity. Current affairs and news stories can also skew results. For example, bad news in the media at the time of a campaign could negatively affect what might otherwise have been a good outcome.

In addition, there is a timing element – some people will respond more quickly to advertising than others. This varies, depending on where they are in the buying funnel, and how long it takes them to take note of and then act on the campaign. Exposure to a multiplicity of advertising methods and contacts also adds to the confusion and difficulty in assigning cause and effect from an individual specific campaign.

Even though it might be hard to record results, and you may not be sure that they are 100% accurate, you should still take some time to figure out what's happening with your campaign. If you can measure something, however approximately, you can work to improve it. It's certainly possible to get some pointers, and even a little guidance is better than none. I always recommend that clients review how their campaigns perform, and encourage them to draw some conclusions from what they find to help them plan for the future.

A view of "success"

It's crucial to have some clear idea about what success looks like – this goes back to the Campaign objectives I talked about in Chapter 3. If you view success as "reaching the objective" that's a great start, but any objective, so long as it is measurable, gives you a way of quantifying your outcomes.

Establishing a base line

Whichever way you choose to start measuring your results, it's essential to define the base line, i.e., where you are before the campaign activity starts.

Without being clear on a common definition of where you are right now, it will be difficult to see what has changed once the campaign activity is over, so record a data reading, to define that base line position early on in the process. Being able to measure something allows you to check its working – even down to the most basic level of "is it on or off?" and to take some view on how to manage it.

Key Measurement Method #1: Product Usage Rate

Sometimes, Promotional Products won't work for a very simple reason – because they never leave the office. This is really basic, and so you can think of this as a reminder.

If you treat Promo Products as a "giveaway" - or just order items without applying them to a campaign where they can work for you – there's a good chance that they will just sit in that stock cupboard in your company Reception area for months on end, and collect dust. If they aren't getting out to their targets, they can't be successful, and that will be a waste of your time, effort, and money, and a bad investment.

So check your stocks - and if for some reason you aren't getting through your Promotional Products at the rate you expected, then someone needs to investigate why.

Here are some possible reasons why your Products might not be reaching their targets.

No distribution plan in place

Maybe there is no plan, it's just "ad hoc" - whoever wants something is free to help themselves.

An informal "campaign" like this needs to be refined and improved to make sure that your people have a method of putting these products into the hands of people you want to use them. Think out of the box for ways to do this – remember, those items are just costing you money if they're sitting in your store cupboard.

The staff don't like them

Could it be that your sales staff are actually embarrassed to give these items to their clients because they don't feel they are appropriate?

Time to get some detailed feedback from your team, and change your product range to include items that they can be proud to carry around and present as gifts to their professional contacts.

Clients are unimpressed

If clients tell you straight out that they don't want your gift, then that's a pretty clear indication of failure.

One of my clients described how embarrassed he was about the lousy quality company pens they were supposed to use (issued from the Head Office) - a seminar guest had even left a feedback form saying "worst corporate pen I have ever used".

Clients are sometimes less direct – but if they leave your gifts behind on their seats at the end of the session, you know something's just not resonating. Or when you're distributing to passers-by at a trade show, perhaps you just can't give them away? If this happens, it's time to review your product choice and make a change.

You could include a feedback form with the gifts you use on your campaigns - you might actually ask recipients about the product itself. This in itself is yet another opportunity for you to ask them to give you an email address if you don't already have it – or maybe another piece of information, like their mailing address or their birthday?

You'll know you've found a good product when you have people asking you if you can spare one more.

How does this help?

The Product Usage Rate is useful to help you check that your basic campaign mechanism is functioning, and that people like your product - however that's about the limit of it – it's not really helping you calculate how much the effort is worth to your company.

Key Measurement Method #2: Campaign Engagement rate

Assuming your products are actually getting out to the clients and prospects you want to reach, then assessing how engaged they are in their response to your campaigns is more useful. You won't necessarily get a hard-cash result from these measurements, but you will get a sense of how well people have responded to your campaign.

Can you actually measure it?

It might seem obvious, but to measure engagement, you'll need your Calls to Action to be related to something you can measure, so remember to incorporate this in the design stage, either on the product itself or on its accompanying paperwork (hangtag, cover letter, packaging, etc.).

Consider campaign objectives such as these:

- Getting your product info into the hands of at least 300 visitors to the trade show.
- Getting an additional 500 Facebook followers.
- Inviting enquiry calls to a specific sales office number.
- Inviting visitors to an event at your showroom.
- Getting hits to your website.
- More signups to a wellness programme.

All these are very achievable objectives for promotional product campaigns, and most of the outcomes are easy to measure.

You can tell if you've achieved your "getting the message to 300 visitors" objective by the end of the day - just count how many of those info banner pens you've got left when the show closes, and subtract that from the number of pens you started with.

Counting responses

It's probably also easy for you to measure increases in the number of Facebook followers from day to day, and to log that on a spreadsheet – the same goes for new subscribers to your mailing list. A rush of visitors to your car showroom one Saturday waving the key fob you sent them will tell you that that promotion achieved its aim of getting then through the door. And you can keep track of calls to a new dedicated phone line easily enough too, provided that you do make sure that's the phone number you print on your Call to Action.

Online Visitors

With the website-related campaigns, it's good to take a little more care in the preparation stage – make sure that you direct people to a unique URL so that you can track visits to that specific page. Otherwise, if they just go to your generic homepage, you will find it difficult to see how many of the total visits are from people who are responding to your campaign. Not only that, you're missing out on the opportunity to customise and personalise the experience for them by rewarding them in some way for their engagement with that particular campaign (Download? Voucher? Coupon? Privileged access to Videos etc?). Check the white paper on this topic, which you can download from our members' page.

How does this help?

Using a combination of the Product Usage Rate and your Campaign Engagement statistics will give you a good idea about whether your campaign is working or not, and help you troubleshoot if something is clearly wrong. However, these measures do not in themselves give you an answer to the question of Return on Investment (ROI), or help you to decide if it's been worth spending the money to get those results.

Key Measurement Method #3: Measuring ROI

As with other types of advertising, Promotional Product Marketing, when executed effectively, does have a positive impact on the process of acquiring new customers. When you combine this with building loyalty from your existing clients and the people who work for your company, you have some of the key elements in place to see profits improve. In the previously mentioned campaign examples, all the objectives described – if achieved – can add "value" to your business.

But how can you actually work out how much value they really add?

If you can assign a $ value to a campaign outcome, then it's possible to get a good way towards understanding that ROI. Don't be fooled by the scientific exactitude of the resultant calculation, though. These assessments won't be exact, because every buying decision is the result of a combination of triggers, contacts, and experiences.

Nevertheless, even simplistic cost-benefit analyses like these will help you budget more accurately for your Promotional Product spending, and help you compare campaigns so that you can select the ones which bring you the best "bang for your buck".

You do need to have a feel for the metrics in your company at the time of your campaign, and that's not necessarily information everyone will have at hand. If it's your own company, you should be able to calculate these, but if you're an employee, you may not be privy to the information. Whatever the situation, if you don't have actual numbers, take action now anyway. Make some initial assumptions (or use what you do know) to start the process with your own analysis, whilst you try to get more accurate numbers to use. Imperfect action beats inaction every time!

Here are some examples of how to assign a cash value to your promotional product campaign outcomes.

Campaigns that directly boost sales

These are perhaps the most straightforward to assess. For campaigns which incentivise purchase directly – e.g., "buy this, get that" campaigns, also known as Gift With Purchase (or GWP) - you simply calculate the additional value of sales achieved using this promotion, and compare that with the cost of the promotional products you bought to make these sales happen.

It's the same if your products are directing recipients to a special offer that is only available at a specific webstore location – again, it's easy to assign a value to the sales you get from the visits that you know can only have been triggered by your campaign.

You can also use the same methodology if you have your clients enter a Special Offer Code unique to your campaign, which you print on your Promotional Product. Whether you take data direct from your webstore or fill in a spreadsheet to track your business sales, just total up the sales value related to that particular code.

Campaigns with non-direct sales objectives

For other types of campaign, where your objective is not to directly trigger a sale, you need to take some extra steps and make some assumptions before you can assign a dollar value to the outcomes.

For example, consider a campaign where the primary goal is to get new email subscribers. New email subscribers could be of very high value to your business – especially if this is your primary method of turning leads into clients.

To do this, start by calculating a Subscriber Value. Take a measure of sales you can attribute to your email marketing, (profit is good, but a sales turnover number is probably easiest for most people to access, and can be equally valid) and divide this by your number of current subscribers to calculate the average value to your business of one subscriber.

If you calculate that your average Subscriber Value is $50 dollars, and you got 30 signups from your campaign, then the incremental value to the business of your campaign is $50 x 30 = total $1,500. Compare that with the cost to you of running the Promotional Product-related campaign required for you to get those sign ups - if the campaign cost less, then that represents a positive ROI.

Campaigns to trigger new Enquiries to your sales team

You probably have a system in place to record and monitor incoming sales enquiries – this could be a manual system, or based on information you collect from your salespeople at a weekly meeting. If you use a CRM system, then you should be able to get this information easily as a standard report.

Take your total sales value for a period, and divide this by the number of new enquiries over the same time. This gives you a simple way to calculate the Average Value of a New Enquiry. If we assume that your Average Value of a New Enquiry is $1,000 and your campaign generated 15 enquiries, this means a total incremental value to the business of $15,000. If the cost of your campaign was less than $15,000, then your campaign has generated a positive return.

Analyse results – making sense of all this.

Keep it Simple

You could argue that these methods are unsophisticated and simplistic measures. I would agree that this is true - I'm the first to admit that the approaches described here hardly scratch the surface of the complexities involved. For example, there is no attempt to take account of changes to money values over time, or of changes in external factors, or changes in the overall operating environment of the business. This is a deliberate ploy to keep all the analysis simple – in my experience, trying to include additional elements causes more confusion, and a whole lot of irrelevant internal debate, and results in "data overwhelm" for most business people.

Basic metrics like these do have the benefit of being accessible and practical - and when used as rough feedback, they are vastly superior to the more common alternative approach – which is to measure nothing.

Trends and comparisons

For meaningful analysis, remember that one result on its own is not really very much help. You should always compare your campaign results with a Baseline Position and look at trends and developments. Your Baseline Position might be before you started using Promotional Product Marketing – this would let you see how much this has helped you. Alternatively, your Baseline Position could be from when you were just using a different incentive - this would let you see how the new Product works in comparison.

Compare the impact on new sign-ups when you offer your new Promo Product. Did that work better than when you were offering people your old Promo Product? Which one gave you the best results?

Review the two campaigns; decide which worked best, and repeat a third time to see if you can improve next time around.

A/B testing is another useful technique. Here you select a variable, and try two alternatives to see which performs best. You can do this simultaneously in smaller test markets or test populations, prior to a larger campaign. Then you compare the results from both, decide which performs best, and then adopt that winning approach for all.

Remember, you are not making exact calculations – you're really looking out for trend patterns, and trying to isolate exceptional or outlying results. Changes in trend or exceptional unexpected results should provoke you to seek explanations and get a better understanding of what's happening, not only with your Promotional Product Marketing campaigns, but also with your overall business situation.

Opportunities for overall performance improvement

If your campaign was designed to trigger engagement - e.g., more calls to request sales meetings – and it suddenly seems to be failing, review what could be the reasons.

Maybe that dedicated phone line has gone down. Or it's the summer holidays and no-one's around to answer it. Or those calls go to a phone that rings on an empty desk somewhere in the office, and no-one's been told to answer it. These things can and do happen!

Be particularly careful when you see unexpected disappointing results – especially when you feel that your campaign has been a success. Sometimes, you need to look a bit harder than just at the nuts and bolts of your campaign – and this might lead you to take action internally to fix a problem which the results throw out, or to find ways to take advantages of new and unexpected opportunities.

If your tradeshow invitation efforts are successful in bringing hundreds of qualified visitors to your stand, but you get a disappointing number of firm interested leads to follow up, your campaign worked, but something else in the process let you down. Look hard to see what the real issues are – maybe you just didn't have enough staff at the booth to handle the volume of traffic. Or maybe there were enough staff, but they had the wrong skill sets for their role at the show, or maybe they need the correct training to be able to book follow-up appointments more effectively.

Here's another situation – maybe you are successful in using Promotional Products to generate more phone enquiries, but you aren't actually seeing the expected increase in sales. Again, perhaps it's a problem of capacity with not enough people in your sales office to handle these new enquiries more effectively. Or maybe, when you start asking questions about this, it turns out that the enquiries generated are mostly for products you don't have in your range, and that has had a negative effect on your sales team's ability to process everything that's coming in.

In cases like this, if your campaign seems to be working in itself, then you can tweak its targeting to get more of what you want. Or maybe you could find a new way for you to supply this unexpected demand, by adding new or additional products to your range?

Going even deeper, maybe you need to review your enquiry handling process to convert those enquiries in another way, perhaps automatically, or by reassigning roles, or getting in some extra help from new staff or freelancers.

In summary

In this Chapter, we've reviewed how marketing metrics are difficult to nail down to hard and fast numbers, whether you want to review historical performance or predict future outcomes. Promotional Product Marketing is no different from other forms of advertising in this sense; however, it can be more accurately targeted than some other methods. It can also be harnessed to create very direct sales responses, and when used this way, there are simple ways to take some measurements. Product usage and campaign engagement are good initial guidelines to check if the basics are working, and there are methods to calculate simple ROI in many cases. Using a range of these metrics can help assess the appropriate levels of spending, spot anomalies in performance, and identify new business opportunities.

Practical Exercise

Now, once again, take five minutes out from reading right now, go to the back of the book, grab a piece of paper, and look through the reminder here of the contents from this Chapter.

Take action now to review each point – and write down the metrics that you could use today to start keeping track of your Promotional Product Marketing activity.

Whether it's that long overdue stock-take you've been thinking about, along with a review of the quantities you've ordered by item over the last three years, or a five minute anything-goes brainstorming of ideas about ways you could measure ROI in your firm, take action now, and apply what we've been talking about to your own situation.

- A view of "success".
- Establishing a base line.
- Key Measurement Method #1: Product Usage Rate.
- No distribution plan in place.
- The staff don't like them.
- Clients are unimpressed.
- How does this help?
- Key Measurement Method #2: Campaign Engagement Rate.
- Can you actually measure it?
- Counting responses.
- Online Visitors.
- Key Measurement Method #3: Measuring ROI.
- Campaigns that directly boost sales.

- Campaigns with non-direct sales objectives.
- Campaigns to trigger new Enquiries to your sales team.
- Analyse results – making sense of all this.
- Trends and comparisons.
- Opportunities for overall performance improvement.

At this stage, you're really well qualified to be the Promotional Product Pro in your organisation, because you'll be able to plan your campaign, select the right products, order them with minimal pain so that they arrive on time, and on spec, and try ways to measure the results of your actions.

Pat yourself on the back, that's a great result!

Now, if you've not already registered for the additional bonus materials and white papers connected to Get Your Name on Cool Stuff, do it now.

Visit www.getyournameoncoolstuff.com

or scan this QR code

and follow the instructions.

CHAPTER EIGHT

Conclusion

So now it's time to act – are you ready to Get Your Name on Cool Stuff?

If you've read this far, you'll know more about the practicalities of Promotional Product Marketing than most of the marketing people you've ever met.

And when you start to apply that knowledge, you'll be well on your way to being a Promotional Products Pro in your organisation.

I've really enjoyed sharing my experience and what I've learned over the years with you through these pages, and I hope you've found it interesting, and maybe even a little inspiring too.

As I said at the start of the book, I'm hoping that this can be a way for us to open a conversation, and for us to get to know each other a little better in a way which allows us to make a connection, and decide if one day it would make sense for us to work together.

I'd really welcome your feedback on the book, or on other aspects of Promotional Product Marketing. And of course, if you'd like me to work with you on your future campaigns, please do get in touch. Feel free to reach out to me at my personal email address here – mark@syncomarketing.com

When done well, Promotional Product Marketing really can make a significant impact to your company's bottom line.

For creative people who like to be challenged and stimulated in practical ways, it's a hugely stimulating area to work in.

But more than anything else, it's really the most fun part of marketing – after all, no-one can resist Cool Stuff!

Last chance!

Now, if you've not already registered for the additional bonus materials and white papers connected to "Get Your Name on Cool Stuff", do it now.

Visit www.getyournameoncoolstuff.com

or scan this QR code

and follow the instructions.

FOR YOUR NOTES

FOR YOUR NOTES

FOR YOUR NOTES

FOR YOUR NOTES